Gardens of the Spirit
Bahá'í Publications Australia
© Copyright National Spiritual Assembly
of the Bahá'ís of Australia Inc.

First Edition 2010
All Rights Reserved
ISBN 1 876322 34 9

Distributed by
Bahá'í Distribution Services
PO Box 300 Bundoora
Victoria 3083 Australia
bds@bahai.org.au
www.bahaibooks.com

Printed in China by
Everbest Printing Co., Ltd

Text by Anita R. Showers
Design and illustration by Monib Mahdavi

Photography
International Bahá'í Community – *Pages: xii, xv, 2, 4 (bottom), 6, 7, 15, 16, 18, 21, 22, 25–29, 31, 34, 35, 38, 42, 43, 46, 47 (left), 48, 49, 51–57, 62, 63, 67, 72, 79, 80, 87, 89, 96, 106, 119, 121, 135, 140, 141, back cover.*

Denny Allen – *Pages: 13, 32, 40, 41, 74, 105, 126 (left).*

Farida Ciotti – *Pages: xvi, 65, 76, 82, 123, 126 (right).*

Koosha Dehghan – *Pages: Cover, 30, 44 (left), 47 (right), 64, 66 (top), 68, 75, 77, 78, 81, 85, 91, 94, 95, 100, 101 (top), 102, 109, 110 (bottom left/right), 111 (bottom left/right), 127 (left), 130, 131 (bottom), 132, 133.*

Monib Mahdavi – *Pages: ii, iii, vi, xvi, 4 (top), 9, 11, 12, 17, 19, 20, 44 (right), 60, 71, 86, 92, 93, 97, 101 (bottom), 103, 104, 108, 110 (top left), 111 (top left), 114, 117, 120, 122, 125, 128, 129, 131 (top), 136, 137, 143, 145.*

David W. Oberst – *Pages: 45, 66 (bottom), 69, 88, 99, 101 (bottom), 116, 118, 127 (right).*

Dedication

With profound gratitude and love to Shoghi Effendi (1897-1957), Guardian of the Bahá'í Faith from 1921 to 1957, who was called the "fresh flower of the garden of sweetness" by his Grandfather, 'Abdu'l-Bahá, and to my dearest mother and grandmother, who cultivated within me an abiding love and appreciation for beautiful flowers and gardens.

Table of Contents

Dedication ... i

Acknowledgements ... vii

Preface ... xi

PART I
The Seeds are Sown ... 1

PART II
The Formal Gardens Unfurl ... 59

PART III
Emergence of the "Floral Jewel" ... 113

PART IV
Flowering in the Future ... 139

vi.

Acknowledgements

I wish to express my deep appreciation to the following individuals who encouraged, inspired, and/or assisted me in various ways toward fulfilling my dream of researching and writing this book: my sister, Doris Phelan; Martha Dick; Tony Burke, Cay Fultz, Brenner Pugh, and Dr. Manouchehr Mohajeri for reviewing the manuscript in assorted stages of development; Dr. Anne Breneman and Bret Breneman for their advice to a first-time book writer; my fellow gardening aficionada, Barbara Payton; my pilgrimage friend, Dr. Dinesh Singh; and Paris Ashton and David Ridderhof for technical contributions.

I am indebted to Denny Allen, Farida Ciotti, Koosha Dehghan, Monib Mahdavi, and David Oberst, for their generosity and beautiful color photographs which adorn this book. I also must convey my gratitude to the National Spiritual Assembly of the Bahá'ís of Australia; Bahá'í Publications Australia, particularly the reviewers, my editor, Nosrat Dehghan, and the designer, Monib Mahdavi; the Secretariat, Research Office, Bahá'í World News Service, Audio-Visual Department, and the Office of Public Information at the Bahá'í World Centre for invaluable guidance and assistance pertaining to historical and current details and photographs; the dedicated gardeners of the past who cultivated the Bahá'í gardens, and the gardeners, horticulturalists, landscape architects, and designers who continue the tradition; and the Universal House of Justice for its protective and loving oversight of the Bahá'í properties.

–*Anita R. Showers*

"Ye are the fruits of one tree, and the leaves of one branch."

— Bahá'u'lláh

Preface

In early April 2005, I stood on "God's holy mountain," Mount Carmel, in Haifa, Israel, surrounded by the most pristine and redolent terraced gardens that I had ever seen.* Below me was a dazzling panorama of the city, the Bay of Haifa, and the ancient prison city of 'Akká in the distance about ten kilometres north**. Above me, centered between nineteen beautifully landscaped terraces, was the stately Shrine of the Báb, the resting place of the Prophet-Herald of the Bahá'í Faith and the One Who foretold the coming of Bahá'u'lláh, the Faith's Prophet Founder.

At the time, I was a Bahá'í pilgrim granted the privilege of visiting this Shrine and other Holy Places of the Bahá'í Faith located in Haifa and 'Akká. While I walked contemplatively along the terraced gardens, my senses were overwhelmed by the awe-inspiring horticultural tapestry of the landscaped terraces cascading with precision down Mount Carmel.

Ma'ariv, one of Israel's most popular newspapers, reported that the Bahá'í terraced gardens in Haifa "have earned the appellation of 'the eighth wonder of the world,'"¹ and rightly so, for they are carved into solid rock, stretch nearly a kilometre up Mount Carmel, and showcase more than three hundred different plantings in a delightful profusion of colors, fragrances, shapes, sizes, and textures. Indeed, the terraced gardens are so stunning in their beauty and meticulous care that the Society of American Travel Writers honored them in 2003 with a Phoenix Award, describing them as "a magnificent floral jewel."²

Admiring that floral jewel as I stood on Mount Carmel, my soul was drawn inescapably to sacred allegorical passages from the Bahá'í Writings, among them...

"...Sow the seeds of My divine wisdom in the pure soil of thy heart, and water them with the water of certitude, that the hyacinths of My knowledge and wisdom may spring up fresh and green in the sacred city of thy heart." ³

The beauty and power of that sublime pilgrimage in the spring of 2005, coupled with my lifelong love of gardens, motivated me to write this book. Since becoming a Bahá'í in 1984, I had awaited the publication of a book about the gardens at the Bahá'í Holy Places, a compilation of the inspiring stories scattered throughout Bahá'í books, memoirs, articles, and official communications from the Bahá'í World Centre. I realized in 2004 that the passion I felt toward this project and my profession in marketing communications conduced to my authoring it. Thus, in 2005 immediately upon returning home from my nine-day pilgrimage to the Bahá'í Holy Places, I began the research in earnest.

---

* Mount Carmel is legendary in the history of the Holy Land and in religious prophecy. Referred to as the "mountain of the Lord" in Isaiah 2:2, the mountain is further praised in Isaiah 35:2, and the prophet Elijah's cave is located on Mount Carmel.

** The spelling 'Akká is used throughout the text. The Hebrew spelling of Acre may appear in captions provided with archival photographs by the Bahá'í World Centre.

The story of the gardens is inseparable from the Bahá'í Faith's history which spans well over a century and a half; hence, I have written this book within the context of that history. The story occurs in what today is Iran, Iraq, Turkey, and the Holy Land of Israel, location of the exquisite gardens at the Bahá'í Holy Places. It is intimately associated with momentous historical events, many occurring in gardens of immense beauty, that surrounded the lives of the Báb and Bahá'u'lláh and Their appointed successors. It is a compelling story about love, selfless devotion, patience, fortitude, and extreme sacrifice, even martyrdom.

The Bahá'í gardens that so many visitors and pilgrims enjoy today bear the indelible imprint of Shoghi Effendi, Bahá'u'lláh's great-grandson and the appointed head of the Bahá'í Faith from 1921 to 1957, who was pivotal in developing the gardens at the Bahá'í Holy Places. He worked tirelessly to overcome tremendous obstacles and to acquire properties near the resting places of the Báb and Bahá'u'lláh in order to ensure the sacredness of the Shrines. The gardens reflect the spirit and genius of Shoghi Effendi, and his countless contributions are detailed in this book.

Moreover, the story of the gardens at the Bahá'í Holy Places in Israel is deeply rooted in the ancient tradition of beautiful gardens in Persia (modern-day Iran), for it was in that country that both Bahá'u'lláh and the Báb were born in the early 1800s. Ancient Persia, one of the oldest civilizations in the world, is where some of the first gardeners originated, as noted in *The Story of Gardening*. Flourishing around 600 AD under the early influences of Islam "... the Persians cultivated fruit trees and flowers, some introduced from Eastern Asia. On the plain around Fars* they grew red roses, exporting the attar (the essential oil produced from them) to India, China, Egypt and the Maghreb."[4]

---

* Fars is a province of Iran located in the southern part of the country. Its capital is <u>Shiráz</u>.

Shoghi Effendi, the Guardian of the Bahá'í Faith, surveying the gardens at Bahjí, 'Akká (Acre), Israel; 1955-1957.

Persians integrated the imagery of gardens and flowers into nearly every aspect of their culture and in virtually all art forms – architecture, engravings, paintings, literature, and especially in the legendary garden carpets of Persia known for their intricate designs of floral images and botanical motifs. In *The Persian Garden: Echoes of Paradise*, the authors note,

"Few people cherish gardens more; in few cultures are its images so pervasive. From the beginning, its water and trees, its flowers and birds informed Persian religion, imagination, language, and arts, and this was so no matter who the ruler or what the belief. It is as if a great flowering vine stretched back through the millennia; blossom, leaf, and tendril unbroken by the swings of a turbulent and often tragic history." [5]

Against this backdrop of rich tradition and the diverse natural beauty of Bahá'u'lláh's native country, this story about the gardens at the Bahá'í Holy Places begins. It is my hope that this book will befittingly commemorate the gardens at the Bahá'í Holy Places for people of all ideologies who have the supreme pleasure of visiting and experiencing the gardens and for those who may never receive that bounty. As well, may this book offer spiritual sustenance and inspire thoughtful meditation to enrich one's soul with the limitless bounties of God.

– *Anita R. Showers, Jan. 2010*

PART I
The Seeds are Sown

A view of the house of Bahá'u'lláh in Tákur, Mázindarán.

e Prophet-Founder of the Bahá'í Faith, (modern-day Iran), a vast country known f splendid, fragrant gardens designed with erchannels to cool the air, and planted ers and blooming trees. Such visually ns served as gathering places for families othing sanctuaries from the oppressive e sun of Persian summers.

Bahá'u'lláh's birth to a family of considerable affluence took place in the country's capital city of Tihrán (now Tehran) on November 12, 1817. At an early age, Bahá'u'lláh was profoundly influenced not only by the beauty of His native country's tradition but also by the beauty of the Caspian Seacoast and nearby northern province along the Caspian Seacoast and nearby forested, mountainous regions.

Persia's immense natural beauty impressed Bahá'u'lláh deeply and engendered a love of nature and gardens that He retained all the years of his life. His eldest son, 'Abdu'l-Bahá, reminisced that His Father, "…was a great lover of outdoor life, most of His time being spent in the garden or the fields.…" Munírih Khánum, the wife of 'Abdu'l-Bahá, recalled that Bahá'u'lláh, "…loved the seas, the hills, and the plains, gardens, flowers, and quick movement in the open air…" Their daughter, Túbá Khánum, remembered that her Grandfather, "…loved gardens, flowers, stretches of country, riding, walking, picnics under the trees, and all open-air simple pleasures."¹

When their children were young, Bahá'u'lláh and His wife, Ásíyih Khánum, often journeyed for pleasure to the province of Mázindarán in northern Persia. Mary Perkins writes in Servant of the Glory: The Life of 'Abdu'l-Bahá:

"Both Bahá'u'lláh and Ásíyih Khánum's family roots were deeply entwined in that province for their ancestors had lived there for many generations. The north of Mázindarán, along the Caspian Sea, was then thickly wooded with ancient forests. Further south, where the Alburz range begins to rise, steep hillsides, where sheep farmers wrest a living, soar above deep green valleys. Tákur, a small village of perhaps 60 households, is situated in a long green valley, two hard days' ride over the mountains from Tihrán.…In Tákur, on a fertile platform of land near a tumbling stream, Mírzá Buzurg, 'Abdu'l-Bahá's Grandfather*, had built a magnificent house and surrounded it with a beautiful garden filled with flowers, fruit trees and flowering shrubs. Here the young 'Abdu'l-Bahá, His sister, Bahíyyih Khánum, and Mírzá Mihdí [their younger brother] spent many happy hours.…On the slopes above Tihrán and in Tákur Bahá'u'lláh shared with His children His own deep delight in the countryside and His love for the beauties of the natural world."²

* Bahá'u'lláh's father

From the published accounts of some early Bahá'ís, it is apparent that whenever time and circumstances permitted, Bahá'u'lláh surrounded Himself and His family with the soul-nourishing beauty and serenity of nature. On many occasions, He visited various gardens in different regions of His homeland, as noted in this account:

"...One year He spent the summer in Murgh-Maḥallih in a garden called 'The Garden of Ḥájí Báqir'. He lived in a three-storey dwelling overlooking a small lake, in the middle of which was a large platform of bedrock encircled with vegetation. At times, a tent would be pitched in the centre of this area, and about one hundred and fifty friends would gather in the small garden surrounding it. The Blessed Beauty* often spoke of this place."[3]

It stands to reason that Bahá'u'lláh's children would inherit their Father's affection for nature and also be influenced by the Persian garden tradition.

His daughter, Bahíyyih Khánum, was described as having, *"...a natural fondness of flowers... that was so characteristic of Bahá'u'lláh."* This same daughter recounted about her own childhood in Persia:

"... We used to go to our house in the country sometimes; my brother 'Abbás ['Abdu'l-Bahá] and I loved to play in the beautiful gardens, where grew many kinds of wonderful fruits and flowers and flowering trees..."[4]

---

* Bahá'u'lláh is often referred to as The Blessed Beauty by His followers.

The house of Bahá'u'lláh in Tákur, Mázindarán, destroyed by the government in 1981.

But beyond the obvious beauty of nature, Bahá'u'lláh recognized that nature reflects the power, mystery, and perfection of God and is one of infinite gifts from our Creator. It is, in fact, in Bahá'u'lláh's Writings revealed during His forty-year ministry, that His deep love of nature and His perfect understanding of nature's divine source find the highest and most meaningful expression. He wrote:

"Nature in its essence is the embodiment of My Name, the Maker, the Creator. Its manifestations are diversified by varying causes, and in this diversity there are signs for men of discernment. Nature is God's Will and is its expression in and through the contingent world. It is a dispensation of Providence ordained by the Ordainer, the All-Wise." [5]

Throughout His extensive Writings, Bahá'u'lláh often explained spiritual truths and virtues by employing botanical imagery such as gardens, flowers, trees, seeds, blossoms, and roses, as well as branches, roots, hyacinths, fruits, leaves, plants, and soil. His Writings are filled with such metaphors, as in this passage about the unity of humanity: *"Ye are the fruits of one tree, and the leaves of one branch."* [6]

'Abdu'l-Bahá, who was appointed by Bahá'u'lláh as His successor, the authorized Interpreter of His Writings, and Center of His Covenant, also graced His Own Writings with allegorical terms of nature to expand on spiritual concepts. He referred to God's successive Manifestations – among them Abraham, Moses, Buddha, Zoroaster, Krishna, Jesus, Muhammad, the Báb, and Bahá'u'lláh – as *"…the divine Gardeners Who till the earth of human hearts and minds."* [7]

In another passage, 'Abdu'l-Bahá allegorically used a seed to illustrate humanity's essential reality:

"We must strive with energies of heart, soul and mind to develop and manifest the perfections and virtues latent within the realities of the phenomenal world, for the human reality may be compared to a seed. If we sow the seed, a mighty tree appears from it. The virtues of the seed are revealed in the tree; it puts forth branches, leaves, blossoms, and produces fruits. All these virtues were hidden and potential in the seed. Through the blessing and bounty of cultivation these virtues became apparent. Similarly the merciful God our creator has deposited within human realities certain virtues latent and potential. Through education and culture, these virtues deposited by the loving God will become apparent in the human reality even as the unfoldment of the tree from within the germinating seed." [8]

Bahá'u'lláh's knowledge of the essence of nature and His love for nature's beauty were also reflected in the symbolic terms of endearment with which He addressed the members of the Holy family. He designated the women as "leaves," bestowing the title of the "Most Exalted Leaf" upon His wife, Ásíyih Khánum (surnamed Navváb), and the title of the "Greatest Holy Leaf" upon His daughter, Bahíyyih Khánum. In some of His Writings, He referred to Khadíjih-Bagnum, the wife of the Báb, as the "Exalted Leaf." He designated the males of His family as "branches," addressing His youngest son, Mírzá Mihdí, as the "Purest Branch," and His eldest son, 'Abdu'l-Bahá, as the "Most Mighty Branch."

'Abdu'l-Bahá, the eldest son of Bahá'u'lláh.

In His *Tablet of the Branch*, Bahá'u'lláh used natural imagery to extol 'Abdu'l-Bahá and alluded to His son's future station:

"Verily the Limb of the Law of God hath sprung forth from this Root which God hath firmly implanted in the Ground of His Will, and Whose Branch hath been so uplifted as to encompass the whole of creation." 9

It was through His deeds that Bahá'u'lláh also expressed His great love of nature. Demonstrating the divine virtues of love, kindness, and generosity, He frequently presented fruit or flowers, usually roses, to those in His presence or would have flowers delivered on His behalf to friends and acquaintances. An early Bahá'í, Tarázu'lláh Samandarí, in his memoirs recounted one such occasion during a Bahá'í festival when Bahá'u'lláh ensured that everyone present was given a fresh red rose:

"…He brought the reading to a close and said, with that heavenly music of His voice: 'Taráz Effendi, stand up!' I stood up. They had brought a quantity of roses from Junayna,* red roses, fresh from the bush, perhaps thirty or forty in all, and placed them on a mat or cushion in His room, on a white cloth. He said, 'Give a rose to each one present here.' I took them up, and I gave one rose to each. Then I stood waiting. He said, 'And what about My share?' I took one and offered it to Him. Then He said, 'Take one yourself, as well.' I took one myself. And He dismissed us, saying, 'Go in God's care – Fí amáni'lláh.'" 10

* *The garden of Junayna, or Junayn, is located in the 'Akká area.*

"Mystically, the pervasive perfume of roses is often unmistakable to some Bahá'í pilgrims who enter the rooms at the Bahá'í Holy Places…"

―――――――――

Anita R. Showers

Along with His companions, Bahá'u'lláh was confined in the pit with His feet in stocks, and encircling His neck were two chains, the weight of which forever scarred His body. In the pitch blackness and squalid atmosphere of that dungeon, Bahá'u'lláh received a vision of the Holy Spirit personified as a Maiden of Heaven who informed Him that He was the One foretold by the Báb. Bahá'u'lláh's Own written account of this divine revelation from God is unique in all of religious history:

"While engulfed in tribulations, I heard a most wondrous, a most sweet voice, calling above My head. Turning My face, I beheld a Maiden – the embodiment of the remembrance of the name of My Lord – suspended in the air before Me.... Pointing with her finger unto My head, she addressed all who are in heaven and all who are on earth, saying: 'By God! This is the Best-Beloved of the worlds, and yet ye comprehend not. This is the Beauty of God amongst you, and the power of His sovereignty within you, could ye but understand.'" 12

After four months of misery in the Síyáh-Chál, Bahá'u'lláh, sick and weak, was released on condition by authorities that He accept banishment from His beloved native homeland of Persia. As His destination of exile, Bahá'u'lláh chose Baghdád, then part of the Ottoman empire and the land once called Babylon. This began a forty-year period of banishments, persecution, and captivity consistently followed by victories, among them, the rooting and flourishing of Bahá'u'lláh's teachings in the hearts of more and more people, and an outpouring of divine revelation – the Word of God – from Bahá'u'lláh in the form of books, tablets, and verses in both Persian and Arabic aimed at promoting unity among the peoples of the world. 13

Exiled for approximately ten years in Baghdád, Bahá'u'lláh lived near the scenic Tigris River and frequently took meditative walks along its bank, partaking of nature's inspiration and beauty. Following some of these walks, He penned sections of *The Hidden Words*, a small book which summarizes the fundamental spiritual teachings of all of God's Manifestations, or Messengers. Also while in Baghdád, He revealed the *Book of Certitude*, in which He expounds upon the spiritual principle that God reveals His guidance to humanity successively through a series of divine Manifestations.

Historical view of Baghdád and the Tigris River.

Although Bahá'u'lláh's inherent knowledge, noble character, and glory earned the respect and admiration of the residents and officials of Baghdád, the Persian government was more determined than ever to thwart future growth of His movement. It persuaded the Sultán of Turkey to banish Bahá'u'lláh even further to Constantinople (now Istanbul).

The people of Baghdád, grief-stricken about His impending exile, came in overflowing numbers to Bahá'u'lláh's house to express their sorrow. The crowds were so large that in order to receive the mass of well-wishers and say farewell, Bahá'u'lláh made arrangements to pitch His tent in the beautiful Garden of Najíbíyyih (also known as the Garden of Najíb Páshá) located across the Tigris River from His house. That beautiful garden of flower-lined avenues was abloom with an abundance of colorful, fragrant roses, and the enchanted singing of nightingales filled the air.

When He arrived in the garden, Bahá'u'lláh made the historic announcement to some of His followers that He was the Promised One foretold by the Báb. The declaration of His divine station transformed a scene of overwhelming sorrow for His family and followers into an occasion of unsurpassed joy, celebration, and triumph. The garden in which Bahá'u'lláh's declaration occurred subsequently became known to His followers as the Garden of Ridván, Ridván being the Arabic word for paradise.

Bahá'u'lláh referred to the first day of His arrival in the beautiful Garden of Ridván as "the Day of supreme felicity" and revealed in a Tablet:

"Arise, and proclaim unto the entire creation the tidings that He Who is the All-Merciful hath directed His steps towards the Ridván and entered it. Guide, then, the people unto the garden of delight which God hath made the Throne of His Paradise." 14

Among the Bahá'ís who were present with Bahá'u'lláh in the Garden of Riḍván was the accomplished Bahá'í historian Nabíl, who wrote this poignant account of those days:

"Every day ere the hour of dawn, the gardeners would pick the roses which lined the four avenues of the garden, and would pile them in the center of the floor of His blessed tent. So great would be the heap that when His companions gathered to drink their morning tea in His presence, they would be unable to see each other across it. All these roses Bahá'u'lláh would, with His own hands, entrust to those whom He dismissed from His presence every morning to be delivered, on His behalf, to His Arab and Persian friends in the city. One night," he continues, *"the ninth night of the waxing moon, I happened to be one of those who watched beside His blessed tent. As the hour of midnight approached, I saw Him issue from His tent, pass by the places where some of His companions were sleeping, and begin to pace up and down the moonlit, flower-bordered avenues of the garden. So loud was the singing of the nightingales on every side that only those who were near Him could hear distinctly His voice. He continued to walk until, pausing in the midst of one of these avenues, He observed: 'Consider these nightingales. So great is their love for these roses, that sleepless from dusk till dawn, they warble their melodies and commune with burning passion with the object of their adoration. How then can those who claim to be afire with the rose-like beauty of the Beloved choose to sleep?'"*[15]

Bahá'u'lláh's stay in the beautiful Garden of Riḍván lasted twelve days. While there, He designated the period from April 21 through May 2 to be commemorated in the future as the Festival of Riḍván in recognition of the magnitude and happiness of the occasion of His declaration. Members of the Bahá'í Faith worldwide celebrate Bahá'u'lláh's historic declaration each year during the twelve-day Festival of Riḍván, the most significant of all Bahá'í Holy Days.

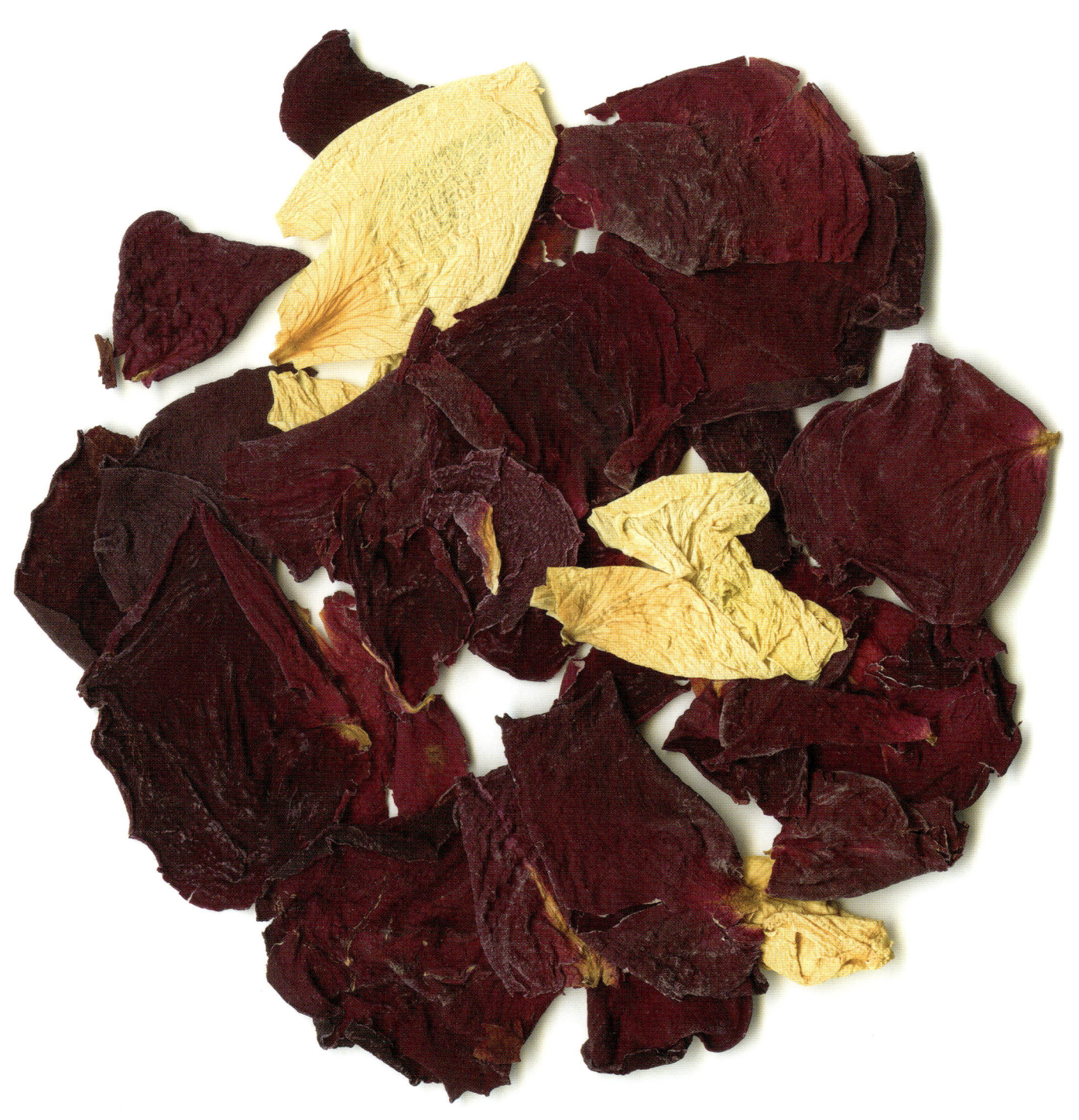

Bahá'u'lláh's residence in Adrianople (Edirne, Turkey) just before His final exile to the prison city of Acre.

Bahá'u'lláh's banishment in 1863 from Baghdád to Constantinople, the capital of the Ottoman empire, was not to be His last. After nearly four months in Constantinople, the authorities hastily exiled Bahá'u'lláh, His family, and companions yet again, this time to Adrianople (now Edirne) on the outermost edge of the empire. The exiles suffered so much during the journey, as they were forced to leave without sufficient provisions and during severe winter weather in which rivers froze and animals in the region perished from exposure.

Bahá'u'lláh and His family lived in Adrianople for almost five years, during which time those opposed to His leadership and majesty made several attempts on His life. Unfazed, Bahá'u'lláh continued to reveal the verses of God. '"Day and night,' an eye-witness has written, 'the Divine verses were raining down in such number that it was impossible to record them.'" 16

In Adrianople, Bahá'u'lláh had occasions to experience the natural beauty of the city and some of its environs. His followers created their own gardens for the enjoyment of Bahá'u'lláh, as noted in H. M. Balyuzi's *Bahá'u'lláh: The King of Glory*:

"In the vicinity of the Muradiyyih quarter there was a piece of land, dotted with trees. Mirza Mahmud-Qulí rented it, and Mirza Mahmud-i-Kashani planted flowers there. In the late afternoon Bahá'u'lláh would repair to that shaded spot, and the companions, returning from their day's work knew where to find Him and attain His presence." 17

One of the residences in which Bahá'u'lláh lived in that city was the house of Rida Big. Regarding this structure and its garden, Balyuzi writes:

"The biruni* had a vast courtyard with a variety of trees and bushes and flowers, and Bahá'u'lláh would occasionally come to the outer quarters, usually late in the afternoon, to pace up and down this garden and speak to the companions." 18

* *The house's outer quarters*

Courtyard of Bahá'u'lláh's residence in Adrianople.

Of foremost significance during His exile in Adrianople, Bahá'u'lláh openly and fearlessly began to proclaim His station through Tablets addressed to particular kings and leaders: the ruler of Persia, Násiri'd-Dín Sháh; the Sultán of Turkey, 'Abdu'l-'Azíz; and Emperor Napoleon III of France. He also revealed a Tablet to the collective kings and rulers of the age. In these unprecedented communications, Bahá'u'lláh urged the sovereigns to champion the causes of justice and peace and cautioned them of dire consequences if they failed to do so.

The outpouring of Bahá'u'lláh's revelation while in Adrianople, the growing number of His followers, and the adoration shown to Him further aroused the jealousy of those who opposed Him. The Sultán of Turkey, reacting to false and malicious accusations spread by those opponents, issued an edict in 1868 which banished Bahá'u'lláh to life imprisonment in 'Akká, a prison city on the Mediterranean coast, now in northern Israel.

The Ottoman empire incarcerated its worst criminals in 'Akká, fully expecting them to die. This fourth exile would, sadly, result in Bahá'u'lláh being deprived for nine full years of even a glimpse of flowers, trees, and the greenery of nature which He so adored.

In Adrianople, Bahá'u'lláh revealed a Tablet replete with natural imagery and specifically addressed to His companions. Adib Taherzadeh in *The Revelation of Bahá'u'lláh* explained:

"*In This Tablet, Bahá'u'lláh portrays Himself as a mystic Rose appearing in the Garden of Paradise. The Rose, the object of adoration of the nightingale, calls out to its lovers to come and be united with the deathless beauty of the Beloved. A few birds resembling nightingales come near the Rose but are not enchanted by its perfume and charm. There is a dialogue between the two which is beautiful and soul-stirring.*" 19

The barracks square of the prison. Bahá'u'lláh was first held in a room adjacent to the square and later moved to His cell on the second floor of the building in the centre of the photo.

On August 31, 1868, Bahá'u'lláh, His family, and about seventy of His followers arrived in the city of 'Akká following an arduous journey by land and sea. They were confined under austere conditions for two years in the city's bleak prison barracks. Bahá'u'lláh suffered greatly during that time, and it was while incarcerated there that His youngest son, Mírzá Mihdí, tragically died from an accidental fall through a skylight in the prison's roof. He was twenty-two years of age.

In October 1870, Turkish soldiers began using the prison barracks for their housing, which made living conditions nearly unbearable for Bahá'u'lláh and His family members, many of them women and children. The authorities decided to relocate the exiles, still under arrest, to a series of houses within 'Akká's fortified walls. The unsightly city offered no gardens and greenery, no opportunity for Bahá'u'lláh to enjoy the outdoors, as He was under strict detention inside His home.

Still, Bahá'u'lláh's revelation of the Word of God continued unabated. He further proclaimed His station through Tablets to additional sovereigns of the time: Kaiser Wilhelm I of Germany, Emperor Franz Joseph of Austria and Hungary, Czar Alexander II of Russia, Pope Pius IX, and Queen Victoria of England. He also issued a second letter to Napoleon III and addressed letters to "the Rulers of America and the Presidents of the Republics therein." Also while confined within the city walls, Bahá'u'lláh revealed the *Kitáb-i-Aqdas*, the *Most Holy Book*, described by Shoghi Effendi as "the brightest emanation of the mind of Bahá'u'lláh, as the Mother Book of His Dispensation, and the Charter of His New World Order."

In the fullness of time, living conditions for the group of exiles eased within the city of 'Akká. Many residents of the city, including some high-ranking officials, eventually conceded that the imprisonment of Bahá'u'lláh and His followers was a grave injustice. The residents, in fact, came to hold Bahá'u'lláh in such high regard that they "…openly asserted that the noticeable improvement in the climate and water of their city was directly attributable to His continued presence in their midst. The very designations by which they chose to refer to Him, such as the 'august leader,' and 'his highness,' bespoke the reverence with which He inspired them." [20]

In June 1877, the authorities at long last permitted Bahá'u'lláh, although still nominally a prisoner, to leave the fortified city of 'Akká and take up residence in the nearby countryside at the Mansion of Mazra'ih.* 'Abdu'l-Bahá described how the transfer of His Father to this property came about:

"Bahá'u'lláh loved the beauty and verdure of the country. One day He passed the remark: 'I have not gazed on verdure for nine years. The country is the world of the soul, the city is the world of bodies.' When I heard indirectly of this saying I realized that He was longing for the country, and I was sure that whatever I could do towards the carrying out of His wish would be successful. There was in 'Akká at that time a man called Muḥammad Páshá Ṣafvat, who was very much opposed to us. He had a palace called Mazra'ih, about four miles north of the city, a lovely place, surrounded by gardens and with a stream of running water. I went and called on this Páshá at his home. I said: 'Páshá, you have left the palace empty, and are living in 'Akká.' He replied: 'I am an invalid and cannot leave the city. If I go there it is lonely and I am cut off from my friends.' I said: 'While you are not living there and the place is empty, let it to us.' He was amazed at the proposal, but soon consented."21

At first, Bahá'u'lláh would not leave the prison city. He was still, after all, a prisoner of the Ottoman authorities; however, He eventually was persuaded to move to Mazra'ih, and the authorities made no objections whatsoever. It is beyond our imagination to comprehend what Bahá'u'lláh must have experienced when arriving at the beautiful Mansion of Mazra'ih after having endured the bleak prison city of 'Akká, devoid of any natural beauty.

In *The Revelation of Bahá'u'lláh*, Adib Taherzadeh notes that Bahá'u'lláh wrote in a Tablet "…about the delightful scenery at Mazra'ih" and in this same Tablet Bahá'u'lláh "…describes in cheerful language the view of the sea on the one side and the hills on the other, and speaks of the charm of the trees laden with oranges which He likens to balls of fire!"22

Bahá'í pilgrims who today visit the Mansion of Mazra'ih walk amid the orange orchards, and breathe in the sweet fragrance of orange blossoms, just as Bahá'u'lláh must have done, admiring colorful roses, other fruit trees, and flowers planted on the beautifully landscaped grounds. Pilgrims also have the honor of praying and meditating in the same room that Bahá'u'lláh occupied on the upper level of the Mansion.

---

* *Mazra'ih is the Arabic word for farm.*

Elevated view of the front (northwest side) of the Mansion of Mazra'ih.

Courtyard of the Mansion of Mazra'ih.

In a Tablet, Bahá'u'lláh described "...the delightful scenery at Mazra'ih."

Bahá'u'lláh wrote "...of the charm of these trees laden with oranges" and compared them to "balls of fire."

In 1877 around the time that His residence was transferred from within the walls of 'Akká to the Mansion of Mazra'ih, Bahá'u'lláh also visited the Garden of Na'mayn, located near 'Akká. This garden was named for the Na'mayn River which flowed nearby. 'Abdu'l-Bahá rented and later purchased this property, which is actually a small island, for His Father's enjoyment and relaxation and arranged to have extensive gardens cultivated there. Bahá'u'lláh's love for the natural beauty of this place and the spirited gatherings held there prompted Him to rename it the Garden of Ridván, in honor of the Ridván Garden in Baghdád where He declared His mission in 1863.

As remembered by Túbá Khánum, the daughter of 'Abdu'l-Bahá, it was always a happy and memorable occasion for everyone whenever Bahá'u'lláh visited the Garden of Ridván:

"Oh the joy of the day when Bahá'u'lláh went to the beautiful Ridván, which had been prepared for Him with such loving care by the Master,* the friends, and the pilgrims!....Only those who were present there could realize in any degree what it meant to be surrounded by such profusion of flowers, their colours and their scents, after the dull walls and unfragrant odours of the prison city. I remember well the greatest of our joys was to go with Bahá'u'lláh for the occasional picnics to the Ridván. How happy we were with Him. He was indeed the brightness of our lives in that time of difficulty." 23

Bahá'u'lláh once wrote that when He entered the Garden of Ridván:

"Every tree uttered a word, and every leaf sang a melody. The trees proclaimed: 'Behold the evidences of God's Mercy' and the twin streams recited in the eloquent tongue the sacred verse 'From us all things were made alive'. Glorified be God! Mysteries were voiced by them, which provoked wonderment....God's power and the perfection of His handiwork could enjoyably be seen in the blossoms, the fruits, the trees, the leaves and the streams." 24

---

* Bahá'u'lláh addressed 'Abdu'l-Bahá as the "Master," a title of respect, and encouraged the Bahá'ís to do the same.

Entrance to the Riḍván Garden in 'Akká (Acre), Israel.

"God's power and the perfection of His handiwork could enjoyably be seen in the blossoms, the fruits, the trees, the leaves and the streams."

Bahá'u'lláh

Fountain in the Ridván Garden in 'Akká (Acre), Israel.

Benches in the Ridván Garden in 'Akká (Acre), Israel.

It was 'Abdu'l-Bahá who ensured that the Garden of Riḍván was maintained with the utmost level of care for Bahá'u'lláh. Knowing of Bahá'u'lláh's love of nature and beautiful flowers, many of the early Bahá'ís also made concerted and devoted efforts to bring Him plants for the Garden of Riḍván.

"…from Persia and neighbouring countries the friends brought many shrubs, trees and flowering plants, some of them rare species. Crossing mountains and deserts, which took several months, they took such care that the plants arrived fresh and ready to be planted in the garden…. They went so far as to bring to 'Akká the plant of a rare white rose which had been one of His favourite flowers in Ṭihrán." 25

Bahá'ís who go on pilgrimage today to the Bahá'í Holy Places spend time in the enchanting Garden of Riḍván. They visit the "little house" where Bahá'u'lláh rested and occasionally stayed overnight and see the exact spot beneath the shade of mulberry trees where Bahá'u'lláh relaxed and took pleasure in the loveliness of the garden. Describing the Riḍván Garden, Túbá Khánum, the daughter of 'Abdu'l-Bahá, recounted:

"Many beautiful blossoming trees are now flourishing there, also flowers innumerable, and sweet-smelling herbs; it is a blaze of glorious colour and wonderful beauty. The scent of attar roses, of rosemary, bergamot, mint and thyme and balm, lemon-scented verbena, and musk makes the air sweet with their wealth of various fragrances. Scented white and scarlet and rose-coloured geraniums are there in wild luxuriance and trees of pomegranate with their large, brilliant scarlet blossoms, also other lovely blooming shrubs. Each a symbol of devoted, loving service. Most of the flowering plants have been brought from Persia by the pilgrims….Some of the gardeners who had been in the employ of Bahá'u'lláh in His glorious gardens at the beautiful country house, His former home in Persia, remembered that a particular white rose was a favourite flower of Bahá'u'lláh's. This rose, single with golden centre, brownish stalks, shiny leaves, and a peculiarly delightful scent, is now flourishing in the Riḍván. Many bushes of these beautiful roses are in full bloom; the waxen cream and gold of their blossoms, and their burnished leaves, make a pure and peaceful note in the love-laden harmony of the glory of that garden." 26

This particular white rose, according to a horticulturalist at the Bahá'í World Centre, may have been *Rosa damascena*, a shrub rose variety long valued for its strong fragrance and suitability in making rose oil; however, this variety is no longer found in the gardens at the Bahá'í Holy Places.

While a number of gardeners over the years maintained the Garden of Riḍván, the first to become caretaker during Bahá'u'lláh's time was Abu'l-Qásim, the subject of this oft-repeated and charming story:

"*One day Abu'l-Qásim saw a thick cloud coming swiftly towards the garden, and in a moment thousands of locusts were covering the tall trees beneath which Bahá'u'lláh so often sat. Abu'l-Qásim hastened to the house at the end of the garden and coming before his Lord besought Him, saying: 'My Lord, the locusts have come, and are eating away the shade from above Thy blessed head. I beg of Thee to cause them to depart.' The Manifestation smiled, and said, 'The locusts must be fed; let them be.' Much chagrined, Abu'l-Qásim returned to the garden and for some time watched the destructive work in silence; but presently, unable to bear it, he ventured to return again to Bahá'u'lláh and humbly entreat Him to send away the locusts. The Blessed Perfection arose and went into the garden and stood beneath the trees covered with the insects. Then He said, 'Abu'l-Qásim does not want you; God protect you.' And lifting up the hem of His robe He shook it, and immediately all the locusts arose in a body and flew away.*"[27]

Abu'l-Qásim's devoted care of the Garden of Riḍván and his warm welcome to all who visited there were well known by the Bahá'ís and deeply appreciated by Bahá'u'lláh, 'Abdu'l-Bahá, and Shoghi Effendi, who was designated the Guardian and head of the Bahá'í Faith after 'Abdu'l-Bahá's passing.

Ugo Giachery, an Italian Bahá'í who assisted Shoghi Effendi with securing marble and other materials needed for construction of the Shrine of the Báb, offered this account in his book, *Shoghi Effendi: Recollections*:

"*…on the evening after my first visit to the Shrine of Bahá'u'lláh and the Mansion of Bahjí, the Guardian asked me what I had first noticed on entering the Mansion… and when I replied that on the wall at the top of the staircase I had seen the framed photograph of an interesting man's head, possibly of a Persian, his [Shoghi Effendi's] face became aglow with an inner feeling of pleasure and gratification. 'Oh, I am glad you did see it,' he said smiling; 'how observant you are. I placed that picture there myself for everyone to see. It is our remarkable and celebrated gardener Abu'l-Qásim, whose services to the Master and myself will never be forgotten.'*"[28]

Today, this framed photograph of Abu'l-Qásim is displayed in its original position on the wall at the top of the Mansion's staircase.

Bahá'u'lláh continued to visit the Garden of Riḍván long after His residence was relocated in September 1879 from Mazra'ih to the Mansion of Bahjí, also near 'Akká. 'Abdu'l-Bahá rented and later purchased the Mansion of Bahjí from its owner who had vacated it when an outbreak of plague erupted in the region in 1879. The larger Mansion would prove to be more suitable in accommodating the increasing numbers of followers who were coming to attain the presence of Bahá'u'lláh.

View of the Mansion of Bahjí and the Shrine of Bahá'u'lláh, 'Akká (Acre), Israel; 1958

The Arabic word "bahjí" means "place of delight." Indeed, this Mansion's spacious interior was delightfully designed, and nestled within the Mansion's outer wall was a small garden. A grove of pine trees stood on the outer property where many picnics and gatherings were held, bringing joy to all who attended them. Today, one of those original native pine trees remains standing at that very location. There were, however, no expansive formal gardens surrounding the Mansion as there are today until Shoghi Effendi designed and developed them decades after Bahá'u'lláh's passing.

Bahá'u'lláh lived for thirteen years at the Mansion of Bahjí. Adib Taherzadeh, author of *The Revelation of Bahá'u'lláh*, writes:

"The prodigious outpouring of the Word of God during Bahá'u'lláh's residence in the Mansion of Bahjí staggers the imagination. The rapidity with which His Tablets were revealed, the manner in which His amanuensis,* …though devoid of a proper education, was empowered by Him to cope with recording His words at an amazing speed, the zeal and enthusiasm with which several of His servants spent long hours every day in transcribing His Writings, all these resulted in the dissemination of innumerable Tablets unprecedented in their range and content during any period of His Ministry." 29

Although still technically a prisoner, Bahá'u'lláh, while living at the Mansion of Bahjí, sometimes left His residence to seek the serenity and pleasure of the natural beauty of 'Akká's outlying countryside. His followers often joined Him to experience the spiritual blessings of His presence and have an opportunity to serve Him. In *Bahá'u'lláh: The King of Glory*, H.M. Balyuzi writes that in addition to the Garden of Riḍván, Bahá'u'lláh also visited…

"…the garden of Firdaws, the gardens of Junayníh and Bustán-i-Kabír at Mazra'ih. He also visited nearby villages, such as Yirkih and Abu-Sinan. At Yirkih, He had His tent pitched on the top of a hill, spending the day in the tent and the night in the village itself. Then there were hills nearer to 'Akká, such as Tall-i-Fakhkhár, which is also known as Napoleon's Hill, and is situated near the Garden of Riḍván…And the hill named Samaríyyih, which overlooks Bahjí and where red flowers grew in abundance, was called Buq'atu'l-Ḥamrá' – the Crimson Spot; today it is occupied by the army. In the springtime when the hill was verdant and covered with red flowers such as poppies and anemones, Bahá'u'lláh would have His tent pitched there. Many years later, when 'Abdu'l-Bahá was again incarcerated within the city walls of 'Akká,** He would wistfully ask those who had gone to visit the Shrine of His Father: 'Were red, red flowers blooming on Buq'atu'l-Ḥamrá'?" 30

---

* Secretary

** After Bahá'u'lláh's passing, 'Abdu'l-Bahá and His family at one point were again strictly confined within the walls of 'Akká by the Turkish authorities who believed false charges made by those opposed to 'Abdu'l-Bahá's appointed station as His Father's successor. 'Abdu'l-Bahá and His family were not officially freed from their exile until the Revolution of the Young Turks in 1908.

When Bahá'u'lláh passed away at the Mansion of Bahjí on May 29, 1892, at the age of seventy-five, His physical remains were buried in a small house adjacent to the Mansion. This is the Shrine of Bahá'u'lláh, the Qiblih* for members of the Bahá'í Faith, and the holiest place on earth for the Bahá'ís of the world. Outside of the Holy Tomb of His Father, 'Abdu'l-Bahá created a small and dignified garden in which mostly citrus trees and flowers were planted. It would be Bahá'u'lláh's great-grandson, Shoghi Effendi, who in later years would adorn the exterior of Bahá'u'lláh's Tomb with formal gardens.

Today, the interior of the Shrine has a small garden of greenery with delicate, wispy intertwining vines that reach upwards toward the skylights, bringing nature, so loved by Bahá'u'lláh and so symbolic of life, inside His earthly resting place. The Bahá'í World Centre notes that this garden may be located on what originally was part of an open courtyard eventually covered by a roof during the ministry of 'Abdu'l-Bahá.

*Arabic for "The Point of Adorations; the direction in which people turn when praying. The Kaaba in Mecca is the Qiblih for Muslims; the Shrine of Bahá'u'lláh at Bahjí is the Qiblih for Bahá'ís." Source: Momen, Wendi, General Editor. A Basic Bahá'í Dictionary, p. 191.

Shrine of Bahá'u'lláh.

Shrine of Bahá'u'lláh and surrounding gardens, Bahjí – 'Akká (Acre), Israel.

Twelve months before His passing, Bahá'u'lláh visited Haifa, one of four excursions that He made to that city, and pitched His tent on Mount Carmel. He pointed out to 'Abdu'l-Bahá the precise place on that mountain below a stand of stately cypress trees where the sacred remains of the martyred Báb, the One who foretold Bahá'u'lláh's coming, should be buried in the future. This directive from Bahá'u'lláh in 1891 was the catalyst for 'Abdu'l-Bahá to take steps over subsequent years to build a suitable tomb for the Báb and eventually would result in the construction of gardens and terraces on Mount Carmel that today are a major tourist attraction in Haifa and visited by millions.

When 'Abdu'l-Bahá heard this divine command from His Father, the Báb's precious remains were, at Bahá'u'lláh's instructions, still hidden in Persia. It was on July 9, 1850, that the Báb and one of His loyal followers were brutally executed by a firing squad in a public square in Tabríz, Persia. This vicious act was the culmination of years of persecution of the Báb and His followers by the fanatical Shí'ih clergy and Persian government. Denied a proper burial, the co-mingled bodies of the Báb and His steadfast companion were thrown outside the city's gate. The second night after the execution, one of the Báb's faithful supporters carried away the sacred remains to a nearby silk factory and placed them in a wooden casket. Subsequently, at Bahá'u'lláh's direction, the casket was hidden at various secret locations in Persia to protect its holy contents from the Báb's enemies.

In 1899, approximately fifty years after the Báb's execution, 'Abdu'l-Bahá arranged for the Precious Dust of the Báb to be brought from Persia to 'Akká and concealed until the Shrine for the Báb was ready. That same year, 'Abdu'l-Bahá set the foundation stone for the Báb's mausoleum on the exact spot selected by Bahá'u'lláh on Mount Carmel, and soon afterwards construction of the Shrine began.

View of Mt. Carmel, circa 1909. The circle of cypress trees marks the place where Bahá'u'lláh stood in 1891, when He indicated the site for the Shrine of the Báb.

Ten years later in March 1909, sixty years after the Prophet-Herald's execution, 'Abdu'l-Bahá, in obedience to His Father's command, laid the Báb's Precious Dust to final rest in the completed one-storey tomb. The elegant gold-domed edifice recognized today as the Shrine of the Báb was added to the original structure and finished in 1953, thirty-two years after 'Abdu'l-Bahá's passing, under the guidance of 'Abdu'l-Bahá's grandson and successor, Shoghi Effendi, himself a relative of the Báb. Today, some of the original cypress trees near the place where Bahá'u'lláh pitched His tent on Mount Carmel are standing directly above the Shrine of the Báb and have always been retained in the design of the gardens near the Shrine.

As noted, 'Abdu'l-Bahá's plan for the Shrine included a garden, which He arranged to have planted even before construction on the Shrine was begun. Ugo Giachery recalled this garden in *Shoghi Effendi: Recollections*:

"I remember having seen, years ago, a photograph taken possibly in 1907 that showed the arrangement of some shrubs and flower plants in front (the north façade) of the Shrine. This garden extended a little to east and west of the building, and was protected by an iron fence of a simple design – perhaps four feet high – and a wood bower at one end, holding up climbing vines. Not much water was then available for the garden, other than that gathered from rain and stored in a cistern, adjacent to the Shrine. This cistern 'Abdu'l-Bahá had built well before the construction of the Shrine was initiated." [31]

'Abdu'l-Bahá's cultivation of the little garden on Mount Carmel prior to construction of the Báb's monument, and His creation of a small garden at the burial site of His Father in 'Akká, instituted a standard of beauty, care, and reverence for the grounds at the resting places of the Báb and Bahá'u'lláh. By establishing this standard, 'Abdu'l-Bahá demonstrated the degree of veneration that even the earth surrounding the Bahá'í Holy Places should receive, thereby forever establishing their spiritual inseparability. This standard was carried forward by Shoghi Effendi and continues to be the guiding compass at the Bahá'í World Centre.

In addition to establishing gardens in the region of the Shrine of the Báb, 'Abdu'l-Bahá also planned to honor the martyred Prophet-Herald of the Bahá'í Faith by creating illuminated terraces from the top of Mount Carmel to its base with the Shrine of the Báb at the center. In this way, 'Abdu'l-Bahá wanted not only to further beautify the sacred burial site of God's Manifestation, but also to provide a suitable path along which pilgrims and visitors would respectfully approach the Shrine of the Báb in the future. The idea for flooding the Shrine and terraces in light, now observable at twilight each evening, was intended as a touching tribute to the Báb, who, for His beliefs and teachings, was incarcerated in 1847 for nine months in the remote fortress of Máh-Kú in northern Persia. About His confinement, the Báb wrote, "… there is not at night even a lighted lamp."32

Likewise, terracing the mountainside would serve a very practical landscaping purpose on Mount Carmel, as explained by Ugo Giachery in *Shoghi Effendi: Recollections*:

*"The rocky and impervious slopes of the mountain presented many difficulties to the habitual gardener, firstly because of limited accessibility, and secondly because of the erosive action of the winter and spring torrential rains which would wipe out any growing thing other than well-rooted trees. The answer, as 'Abdu'l-Bahá had anticipated, was terraces that would retain the soil and provide level ground on which to plant flowers and shrubs."*33

'Abdu'l-Bahá successfully completed one basic terrace at the Shrine of the Báb before He passed away on November 28, 1921, in Haifa. His remains were interred in one of the rooms inside the Shrine of the Báb. In His Will and Testament, 'Abdu'l-Bahá appointed His eldest grandson, Shoghi Effendi, then only twenty-four years of age, as Guardian of the Bahá'í Faith and head of the worldwide Bahá'í community.

Shoghi Effendi made a commanding imprint on beautifying and expanding the gardens at the Bahá'í Holy Places. Foreshadowing that role, 'Abdu'l-Bahá touchingly referred to His grandson, then only a small child, as "the fresh flower of the garden of sweetness."34 'Abdu'l-Bahá also tenderly described Shoghi Effendi with terms of natural imagery in a prayer that He revealed for this adored grandson, invoking the designation of "branch" that Bahá'u'lláh had used long ago for the males of His family:

*"O God! This is a branch sprung from the tree of Thy mercy. Through Thy grace and bounty enable him to grow and through the showers of Thy generosity cause him to become a verdant, flourishing, blossoming and fruitful branch."*35

The Shrine of the Báb with rooms added by Shoghi Effendi, 1939.

Mount Carmel, circa 1909. The Shrine of the Báb can be seen half way up the mountain, with the cypress trees at the back left of the structure.

Looking down towards the small gardens immediately surrounding the Shrine of the Báb, Haifa, Israel; 1936.

Gilded peacocks embellishing the precincts of the Shrine of the Báb; 15 March 1953.

The octagon of the Shrine of the Báb, with its pinnacles and balustrade, during additional construction in 1952.

PART II

The Formal Gardens Unfurl

During Shoghi Effendi's thirty-six year tenure as Guardian of the Bahá'í Faith and head of the Bahá'í world community, the gardens at the Shrines of Bahá'u'lláh and the Báb underwent extensive development and beautification. At the time when Shoghi Effendi began his Guardianship, the gardens at the Shrines were small yet dignified creations begun by his Grandfather, 'Abdu'l-Bahá, Who also had devotedly supervised their care.

Shoghi Effendi wasted no time on his mission to develop and further beautify these original gardens. He set about his task using systematic methods that are recounted in detail by his wife, Rúhíyyih Rabbaní,* in *The Priceless Pearl*, her biography about the Guardian, and by his long-time aid and friend, Ugo Giachery, in *Shoghi Effendi: Recollections*. Before reading their accounts of what and how Shoghi Effendi remarkably accomplished with the gardens, it is pertinent to note that the Guardian had no formal training as a landscape architect. What he did possess in his heart, however, was his beloved Grandfather's standard of beauty and reverence for the gardens and 'Abdu'l-Bahá's mandate for creating illuminated terraces to be constructed at the Shrine of the Báb. As well, he possessed a great love of nature and gardens and knew of the Persian garden tradition, all of which he inherited from both Bahá'u'lláh and 'Abdu'l-Bahá. That Shoghi Effendi gardened with a keen sense of tradition and history cannot be denied.

Rúhíyyih Rabbaní's description of how the gardens at the Shrine of the Báb were developed by the Guardian follows:

"...*Shoghi Effendi studied the surrounding barren mountain side and began to develop, piece by piece, year after year, separate sections. With the exception of the terraces it must be borne in mind that he never had an overall plan. This is what gives the gardens on Mt. Carmel their unique character. As he walked about, Shoghi Effendi would get an idea for a piece of garden that fitted the topography of the land. With no fuss, no advice and no help except the unskilled farmers who did duty as gardeners, he would make his plan for this 'piece'. If necessary he would have the spot surveyed and curves or long lines laid out, but very often he dispensed with this and did it all himself.... When he had it all planned, he would go and stand and instruct the gardeners how to lay it out. Through string tied to pegs, giving long lines, a peg and string acting as a compass for circles, using the span (the space between thumb and little finger when fully stretched apart) as measurement of distance between trees, having light-coloured soil poured out to indicate a line, and other such simple methods he would, often in a single afternoon, have an entire section of garden laid out in full detail. Usually, knowing exactly what he intended to do, Shoghi Effendi would call other gardeners to follow along behind those that were laying out the design, so that as the plan was measured out on the ground, holes for cypress trees were dug, trees planted, flower beds set out and borders planted, all while Shoghi Effendi advanced with his measuring process in front of them!*"[36]

---

* Married to Shoghi Effendi from 1937 until his passing in 1957, Rúhíyyih Rabbaní was also Shoghi Effendi's personal secretary during his Guardianship. Rabbaní is the surname of Shoghi Effendi. He later gave her the title Amatu'l-Bahá Rúhíyyih Khánum, meaning "Handmaiden of Bahá." She passed away in January 2000, in Haifa, and her remains were laid to rest in a small garden. See page 141.

Star designs on the slope of the mountain above the International Archives Building, Haifa, Israel; 1950s circa.

Shoghi Effendi views the Shrine of the Báb from the top of Mount Carmel.

Star-shaped flower beds and statuesque cypress trees, as shown near the Shrine of the Báb in Haifa, are distinguishing features of the Baháʼí gardens.

Elaborating on the Guardian's resourcefulness and diligence in completing the gardens on Mount Carmel, Ugo Giachery wrote:

"*Shoghi Effendi... had the rare capacity to visualize things as a whole after a plan had been conceived by him. When the possibility of erecting the superstructure of the Báb's Sepulchre seemed about to materialize, Shoghi Effendi intensified the landscaping of the surrounding grounds. Much inventiveness and imagination were required to adapt to the irregular nature of the ground the superb and graceful landscaping he planned, to make a befitting framework for the majestic structure of the Shrine when it would be completed. Therefore from the inner recesses of his refinement and good taste and from the natural resources at hand, with his usual enthusiasm, he drew the arrangements of colours, plants, flowers, trees and shrubs that make up the beautiful gardens on Mt. Carmel. I saw him intensely at work, directing a few men to trace lines, stretch strings, place a plant here and there, or a pedestal or an ornament, to lay out, from the first moment, what would be stable and permanent. I cannot remember having heard him once say, "Take that away", or "remove" this or that. There was always an air of contentment and gratification radiating from his dear face...*"37

"An enchanting garden filled with an atmosphere of life, of love and of sanctity" surrounds the burial places of Bahá'u'lláh's wife and youngest son on Mount Carmel in Haifa.

Additional landscaping near the Monument Gardens took place in the 1950s when the gardens around the planned Baháʼí International Archives building on Mount Carmel were developed in a most creative way by Shoghi Effendi. At the time, many were completely astonished that he planted the gardens for the Archives building before construction of the edifice commenced, as explained by Rúhíyyih Rabbaní in *The Priceless Pearl*:

"First he spent much time in studying, through strings laid out on the ground marking the dimensions of the building, the exact position he wanted it to occupy, which he changed a number of times until he was satisfied with its location; he then proceeded to landscape all the area in front of it, laying out paths and planting trees and lawns. He then informed Leroy Ioas, who was to supervise the work…that the building would have to be built from the rear, fitting the front into the gardens that already surrounded it….The result of this was that as the edifice rose, it rose in a setting of gardens which appeared well-grown and mature and when it was completed, far from having that usual desolate stretch of tramped down land around it, it looked as if it had been standing there for years." [41]

During one of His excursions to "God's holy mountain," Baháʼu'lláh revealed the *Tablet of Carmel*, a significant and mystical Tablet in which He alluded to the future establishment on Mount Carmel of the World Centre of the Baháʼí Faith. Land in the shape of a semicircle, or arc, and located to the east of the Archives building and above the Monument Gardens was later designated by Shoghi Effendi as the site in the future for additional buildings intended for the Baháʼí administration, as ordained by his Great-Grandfather.

On this arc-shaped stretch of land, Shoghi Effendi cultivated extensive gardens dominated by statuesque cypress trees, expansive green lawns, and distinctive eight-pointed star-shaped flower beds, which still adorn those gardens today, just as Shoghi Effendi originally created. This garden, when first planted, was described by Rúhíyyih Rabbaní as sweeping "…up the mountain in swirls like the gourd motif on a paisley shawl." [42] The beautiful gardens are directly in front of several administrative buildings, which together with the Baháʼí Holy Places in Haifa and 'Akká, constitute the Baháʼí World Centre.

View of the Arc path stretching from east to west. Another path at the base bisects the Arc into north and south, which situates the Monument Gardens. Haifa, Israel; 1955-1958.

As directed by Shoghi Effendi, the gardens in front of the Bahá'í International Archives building were planted before construction of the edifice began, to the astonishment of many. When the building was completed in 1957, the landscaping was well-established and "looked as if it had been standing there for years."

Formal gardens that surround the final resting place of Bahá'u'lláh in Bahjí evolved from a small garden devotedly created in the early 1890s by His eldest son, 'Abdu'l-Bahá.

During his Guardianship, Shoghi Effendi dedicated no less attention and love to honoring his Great-Grandfather, Bahá'u'lláh, by completely transforming the outlying property at His resting place in Bahjí into a virtual garden paradise. The formal gardens at the Mansion of Bahjí near 'Akká have their genesis in a small garden which 'Abdu'l-Bahá created at the resting place of His Father after Bahá'u'lláh's passing in 1892.

'Abdu'l-Bahá gave this little garden at the Shrine of His Father much devoted care throughout His lifetime. Adib Taherzadeh in *The Covenant of Bahá'u'lláh* relates the following from personal recollections of early Bahá'ís:

"Hájí Mírzá Haydar-'Alí recalls many scenes in which 'Abdu'l-Bahá was seen to be carrying heavy vessels of water on His shoulder for watering the flowers and shrubs in the garden around the Shrine. So strenuous was this task for the Master that sweat could be seen pouring from His face as He carried this heavy burden. The same chronicler has recounted that on several occasions, He was seen gathering soil, placing it inside His cloak and carrying the load on His shoulders to where He was making some flower-beds in the small garden He had created with His own hands in order to beautify the approaches to the Holy Shrine. Dr Habib Mu'ayyad, another faithful secretary of 'Abdu'l-Bahá, writes in his memoirs that when a few years later a mechanical pump was installed in the garden near the Shrine, 'Abdu'l-Bahá used to pump water from the well with His own hands. Dr Mu'ayyad recalls that on a certain day in 1914, 'Abdu'l-Bahá, who was then seventy years of age, moved the handle of the pump for 19 minutes non-stop and stored a great deal of water for later use in the gardens!"[43]

While traveling in India, Rúhíyyih Rabbaní once reminisced that later in His life:

"'Abdu'l-Bahá used to come on foot two miles in the heat carrying flower pots on His shoulders. He was an old, old man with white hair and white beard and He used to carry these flower pots to the tomb of Bahá'u'lláh from one of the gardens in order to plant them near the tomb of His Father."[44]

Shoghi Effendi patiently waited many years to complete his goal of further beautifying the gardens at the resting place of Bahá'u'lláh as well as restoring the Mansion of Bahjí, as there were innumerable delays and obstacles to overcome to gain title to properties near the Mansion. For example, immediately after Bahá'u'lláh's passing in 1892, a small group of individuals who contested and sought to undermine the leadership of Bahá'u'lláh and 'Abdu'l‑Bahá continued to live in the Mansion of Bahjí and a few houses within close proximity. These tenants failed to maintain the Mansion, and its roof eventually caved in from neglect.

In time, circumstances enabled Shoghi Effendi to pursue ownership of the Mansion and the immediate property, which he accomplished in 1929, and soon after he initiated the complete restoration of the Mansion. Over several decades, Shoghi Effendi acquired additional land adjacent to the Mansion and was able to begin in the early 1950s the systematic design and development of the formal gardens at the Mansion and Shrine. Ugo Giachery describes the general condition of the Mansion's outlying property prior to this transformation:

"*Once the evacuation of the occupants of the Mansion and its restoration had been achieved, Shoghi Effendi immediately began to direct his efforts to beautification of the little land available and particularly of the small plot to the north and west of the Shrine, and of the strip enclosed between the wall of the Mansion's garden and the east side of the Shrine and the building used as an early pilgrim house. Araucaria and tangerine trees were first planted*

there, with a few cypress and orange trees in front of the Shrine…. The rest of the grounds a few metres away and all around the building, was a sea of sand, in some places actually dunes, while at about one hundred and thirty metres' distance, opposite the door of the Sepulchre, there was a large deep pit, possibly excavated a long time before to obtain sand for building purposes. On the west side, and at the rear of the Shrine, there were some olive trees, a few eucalyptus trees, and some ancient pines, which at the time of Bahá'u'lláh's residence in the Mansion were the only source of shade and coolness, during the torrid heat of the long Palestinian summers. This was the condition of the grounds around that Blessed Spot when I first saw it."[45]

View of Bahjí showing the balcony of the Mansion, the Shrine of Bahá'u'lláh, and the Pilgrim House; 1910-1920 circa.

Shrine of Bahá'u'lláh, Bahjí – 'Akká (Acre), Israel; 1923.

Shoghi Effendi designated the finished formal garden as the Ḥaram-i-Aqdas, or the "Most Sacred Precincts," thereby incorporating the concept of inseparability of the Shrine and its grounds.

"By the end of the fourth day, the sacred precincts...had taken on the appearance of a beauteous, entrancing garden, looking as if it had been there from ancient times, and much as we see it today...."

Ugo Giachery

Transforming the grounds into formal gardens befitting the resting place of God's Manifestation was the weighty challenge then faced by the Guardian. It is unknown how much prayerful time and strategic thought he actually devoted to crafting the design and layout or procuring the flora to begin the project; however, from a vivid written account from one who assisted Shoghi Effendi with the work, we have a sense of the determination, devotion, and vision that over the course of one week forever altered that pitted earth and "sea of sand". Ugo Giachery writes:

"One evening, Shoghi Effendi came to the dinner-table with an expression of inner joy and determination on his face. After the usual greetings and before we started our meal, he looked around and said: 'Early tomorrow morning we all shall go to Bahjí: I am asking every available man to be there, as we have some very important work to do.' This was the beginning of one week of intense labour which completely changed the nature and aspect of the grounds – already described as a 'sea of sand' – into a garden and paradise of incomparable beauty.

"The reader can hardly imagine, what took place in those blessed days. All able-bodied men were there at the appointed hour. Shoghi Effendi with his mastery skill, already demonstrated in his beautification of the surroundings of the Shrine of the Báb, followed a plan preconceived in his mind. Assisted by his chauffeur who carried a ball of string and some wooden pickets, he traced all the paths, nine in number, which like a fan were to radiate from the Shrine of Bahá'u'lláh towards a semicircular line…

"Guided by the strings which marked the paths, some of the gardeners dug small trenches in which to plant hedges of thyme. The widest path was the one leading from the 'circle' to the door of the Shrine of Bahá'u'lláh.…A group of small dilapidated buildings cluttering the south end of the space between the Mansion of Bahjí and the Shrine was in no time torn down and the stone used to build a level platform in front of the Mansion on the side of the main entrance. Everyone was working with alacrity and high spirits as we were conscious of the process of purification of that holy ground – often blessed by the presence of God's Manifestation – and of the creation of the 'Ḥaram-i-Aqdas', to surround forever that Most Sacred Spot.…I was helping Shoghi Effendi with the tracing of the paths and the star-shaped flower beds.… Shoghi Effendi was moving about directing, counselling, encouraging, explaining, demonstrating how to do apparently impossible things, and rejoicing in the transformation of the land under our very eyes. In the afternoon a drizzle came down but he would not leave the grounds, determined to accomplish as much as was possible before sunset. Markers and trees placed by the previous owners, who had never permitted either the purchase of the land or extension of the gardens around the Shrine, were removed. Young trees were brought in and planted along the paths; the outer semicircular line was doubled to make a wide tree-bordered avenue. Iron gates, steps, stone decorations, flowering plants, top soil and grass seeds were brought from Haifa, from Mt. Carmel, the Riḍván Garden and the Master's House to give consistency to the superb embellishment plan.

"During the night Shoghi Effendi developed a cold, but in the morning he returned to work, feverish and suffering from all the inconvenience brought by the rheum. For three additional days he did not give up; there was ground to level, trees and borders to plant and a hundred other details, all well established and correlated in his mind, and which only he would be able to accomplish. The sand was disappearing; the stones from the demolished buildings were already covered with good soil; hedges, pedestals and flowerbeds were in place, and the neglected area which for over half a century had been a scourge to the sanctity of the Holy Tomb was not only cleansed and purified but had acquired also the beauty and the fragrance of a true 'Holy Court'…

"By the end of the fourth day, the sacred precincts of the Qiblih of the Bahá'í world had taken on the appearance of a beauteous, entrancing garden, looking as if it had been there from ancient times, and much as we see it today."[46]

Visitors and Bahá'í pilgrims frequently inquire about the symbolism of the gardens' ornamentation, such as this eagle which represents strength and victory.

View from the balcony of the Mansion of Bahjí, 'Akká (Acre), Israel.

Blooming and evergreen trees, emerald lawns, and flower beds shimmering with color adorn the gardens adjacent to the Shine of Bahá'u'lláh.

Rúhíyyih Rabbaní also described the property's conversion:

"…when he [Shoghi Effendi] saw a drawing, or had worked out himself his dimensions, studying his terrain, his proportions were absolutely perfect. It is the combination of this sense of proportion, and an originality unhampered by tradition or too much information, that made his gardens so unique, so fascinating and beautiful.…Nowhere was this more manifest than in his development of the grounds surrounding the Shrine of Bahá'u'lláh at Bahjí. His original plan was to have the Holy Tomb and the adjacent Mansion, the hub of a great wheel. He started, after the final transactions were completed with the State of Israel and over 145,000 square metres of land was [sic] secured around the Holy Tomb in 1952, to level the section of wilderness, constituting about one-quarter of a vast circle, that faced the Shrine. A bulldozer was hired and for many days Shoghi Effendi took up his residence in Bahjí, in order to personally direct the work." [47]

As noted, Shoghi Effendi designated the finished formal garden as the a, or the "Most Sacred Precincts," thereby incorporating the concept of inseparability of the Shrine and its grounds instituted by 'Abdu'l-Bahá. In his writings, Shoghi Effendi refers to the Haram-i-Aqdas as the outer sanctuary of the Shrine of Bahá'u'lláh. It comprises approximately a quarter-circle, or quadrant of land, which is located to the north and west of the Mansion and encloses the Shrine.

Many Bahá'ís are familiar with the story of the little one-room building on the outer edge of the property at Bahjí which was originally a utility building for nearby olive groves. Shoghi Effendi would climb onto the building's rooftop and from the elevated height inspect the work on the gardens. Viewing them from this perspective, according to Rúhíyyih Rabbaní, inspired him to terrace a portion of the gardens:

"…as a great deal of earth was being scraped up in the levelling process he instructed that this should all be pushed to the east, and a high embankment was raised there, enabling anyone standing on it to see the whole area stretched before him like a beautiful patterned carpet. The success of this plan pleased the Guardian so much that he built not one but two stepped-back terraces, amounting in height to a small hill.…After his passing, in fulfillment of his own expressed intention, a third terrace was raised on the other two, placing the final touch on his magnificent arrangement of the Shrine gardens. This new concept meant that his original cart-wheel design of gardens was entirely abandoned, for the system of converging paths on a common centre was no longer feasible." [48]

Ugo Giachery also provides this account about the development of those same terraces at the Mansion of Bahjí:

"The following year, when the spring rains came in deluge, lashing the grounds under a strong north-east wind, a good part of the new garden was flooded. This called for an immediate remedy and Shoghi Effendi had the answer ready. Why not build a sort of impediment in the form of an embankment which would prevent the rain water from settling in the gardens? This first embankment took the form of a mortarless terrace, which became an excellent point of observation. This so pleased the Guardian that he added a second one and made plans for the third, which was not completed until after his passing. Gates and steps were made available to allow visitors to climb to the very top, with three broad paths, one on each terrace, which were bordered with cypress trees…In no time the side of the terraces looking toward the Shrine were landscaped with row upon row of geraniums, making the earth appear as if on fire with their innumerable red-flaming blossoms." [49]

Today, visitors and Bahá'í pilgrims can stroll along the terraces, surrounded by towering cypresses and thousands of blooming red geraniums, and from that vantage point can view the expansive garden – the "beautifully patterned carpet" – that extends outward from the Mansion of Bahjí and the Shrine of Bahá'u'lláh.

From the rooftop of this one-room building, Shoghi Effendi inspected progress on construction of the gardens at Bahjí.

Flame-red geraniums were a signature flower in the gardens during Shoghi Effendi's tenure as Guardian of the Bahá'í Faith and are ever-present today along paths and terracing.

Due to Shoghi Effendi's untimely death while in London on November 4, 1957, he was unable to complete his final plan for the property – to remove certain dilapidated buildings nearest the Mansion of Bahjí and finish the garden – but this was accomplished soon after his passing, as recalled by Rúhíyyih Rabbaní:

"It had been the expressed desire of the Guardian himself to supervise the demolition of these houses that abutted on the Mansion and were right next to the Shrine, but he never returned to the Holy Land. When, in fulfillment of his own plan, they were pulled down a few months after his passing, it was found that the large formal garden he had made in front of them was so accurately measured out and planned that it could be continued – I am tempted to say rolled out like a carpet – with complete accuracy right over the place where they had stood and up to the very wall of the Mansion." 50

This beautiful expanse of garden, rectangular in design, resembles a colorful horticultural carpet and especially so when viewed from the Mansion's balcony on the second level. The myriad plant varieties growing in the garden and the overall design create a spectacular pattern.

Shoghi Effendi also created a unique indoor garden on the second floor of the House of 'Abbúd in 'Akká. A Bahá'í Holy Place visited by Bahá'í pilgrims, this house was one of several in which Bahá'u'lláh and His family lived while confined within the fortified walls of the prison city. Rúhíyyih Rabbaní explained how Shoghi Effendi developed this charming garden in the house's second-floor courtyard:

"Not asking any advice – and consequently not being advised not to – he proceeded, with extra tiles, a little cast cement work, an old wooden pedestal, a metal peacock and a few plants, to create a tiny square of garden that was not only charming but drew the wandering inhabitants of 'Akká – who visited the house on the days it was open to the public – to stare at it open-mouthed, a new and unheard of thing…"[51]

This small enchanting garden, planted with succulents and evergreens, today offers an unexpected and delightful greeting to those who ascend the staircase to the upper level of the house.

For the formal gardens at the Shrines, Shoghi Effendi deliberately chose an array of flower, shrub, and tree species displaying a palette of colors, textures, sizes, shapes, and fragrances. The species of plants he selected also were native to many different countries. Rúhíyyih Rabbaní recalled:

"In the first ten years or so of his ministry Shoghi Effendi did everything in his power to ensure that the effects produced by those plants he admired in other countries should be reproduced in his own gardens in the Holy Land…"[52]

The Appendix in *Shoghi Effendi: Recollections* includes a list of the various species of trees, shrubs, vines, and hedges, flowers, grasses, succulents, and cacti that Shoghi Effendi planted in the Bahá'í gardens. Ugo Giachery noted that many of the plants were indigenous to Israel, well-suited to their native habitats and requiring less watering, and that many were original to the Mediterranean area, Africa, America, Australia, and the Pacific Islands.[53]

Shoghi Effendi selected these myriad plantings to co-exist perfectly within the cohesive design of the gardens and to symbolize the spiritual principle of the oneness of humanity with its beautiful diversity of peoples and cultures. This principle of unity in diversity – a central principle of Bahá'u'lláh's revelation – is evident today in the hundreds of different types of flowers, trees, and shrubs which thrive in perfect harmony and balance in the gardens at the Bahá'í Holy Places, especially at the Shrine of Bahá'u'lláh and the terraced gardens at the Shrine of the Báb.

"These were the product of the foresight of Shoghi Effendi, whose sagacity had envisioned the ideal beautification of the landscape around the Holy Places of the Faith."

Ugo Giachery

Visitors to the Bahá'í gardens in Haifa and 'Akká today cannot help but notice the stone-covered winding paths designed to be both functional and a colorful artistic element of the overall garden landscaping. The crushed red tiles on the paths in the gardens at both Bahjí and on Mount Carmel were, according to Shoghi Effendi's wife, similar to the "deep red-coloured paths" which Shoghi Effendi had observed at Babbacombe downs at Torquay, England, a sea resort. She wrote:

"Many years later we were to go there together, and I was shown the famous Babbacombe downs by the Guardian and we walked in the park he had visited so long before – a park with deep red-coloured paths which I believe were the very ones that impressed upon his mind the beauty of red paths and green lawns and ornamental vases in conjunction and inspired him years later to duplicate them in his own beautiful gardens at Bahjí and on Mt. Carmel." 56

Ugo Giachery also wrote about these paths in *Shoghi Effendi: Recollections*:

"…of interest is the varied colour of the paths; some are bright white, filled with pebbles from the Sea of Galilee, while others are ochre-red, covered with crushed roof tiles of French manufacture….Shoghi Effendi, whose talent for originality was immense, devised the idea of alternating paths of different colors in the gardens, and kept on buying discarded roof tiles – from demolished houses or other sources – and having them crushed into small fragments by an ingenious, hand-operated, small machine. In the late 'fifties, however, the supply of red tiles became scarcer and scarcer, and crushed bricks were used as a substitute." 57

When walking in quiet reflection in the Bahá'í gardens, one can easily become enchanted by the cadence and characteristic crunching sound of feet making contact with the white stones and crushed red tiles along these paths. Shoghi Effendi and millions of others throughout the world have themselves strolled along some of these very paths, no doubt charmed by that same distinctive sound and by the overall artistic beauty of the colored paths against the lush green of grassy lawns.

"...in ancient Persian literature the peacock was considered the symbol of eternal life, while the eagle he considered the symbol of victory."

Ugo Giachery

The gardens at both Bahjí and at the Shrine of the Báb are decorated with a variety of ornamental art, much of which Shoghi Effendi planned and purchased. In his memoirs, Ugo Giachery described them:

"They include vases, obelisks, urns, fountains and birds, placed on pedestals of dressed local stone or of Carrara marble. Some urns are beautiful examples of Italian carving; others are reproductions of peacocks, eagles, or flowers – mostly tulips – made of pewter or other lead alloy, which Shoghi Effendi purchased from time to time in Europe. They are fine works of art endowed with graceful elegance which add considerably to the beauty and magnificence of the gardens surrounding the Shrine….Visitors or pilgrims would often ask the meaning of peacocks and eagles situated in the proximity of the Shrine….The beloved Guardian, at times much amused, always infinitely patient, would explain how in ancient Persian literature the peacock was considered the symbol of eternal life, while the eagle he considered the symbol of victory."[58]

Visitors and Bahá'í pilgrims who tour the gardens today frequently inquire about the symbolism of this very same ornamentation.

Objects that adorn the gardens "…are fine works of art endowed with graceful elegance which add considerably to the beauty and magnificence of the gardens surrounding the Shrine…."

PART III

Emergence of the "Floral Jewel"

DECEMBER 1971:

> GARDENS BAHJÍ HAIFA EXTENDED BY DEVELOPMENT QUADRANT SOUTHEAST MANSION BAHÁ'U'LLÁH AND ESTABLISHMENT FORMAL GARDEN SOUTHWEST CORNER PROPERTY SURROUNDING SHRINE BÁB.[59]
>
> UNIVERSAL HOUSE OF JUSTICE

DECEMBER 1973:

> REJOICE ANNOUNCE FRIENDS BEAUTIFICATION DURING CONFLICT AGITATING MIDDLE EAST FOURTH QUADRANT AREA SURROUNDING MOST HOLY SHRINE EMBRACING OLIVE GROVE SOUTHWEST PILGRIM HOUSE BAHJÍ BLESSED SHRINE AND MANSION NOW COMPLETELY ENCIRCLED BEAUTIFUL GARDENS INSPIRED BY PATTERN HARAM-I-AQDAS CREATED BY BELOVED GUARDIAN.[60]
>
> UNIVERSAL HOUSE OF JUSTICE

SEPTEMBER 1980:

> WITH HEARTS BRIMMING WITH GRATITUDE FOR BOUNTIFUL CONFIRMATIONS BLESSED BEAUTY ANNOUNCE FOLLOWING RECENT ACCOMPLISHMENTS HOLY LAND: IN BAHJÍ JUST ACQUIRED STRIP OF LAND 13,150 SQUARE METRES IN AREA BORDERING DRIVEWAY FROM WESTERN GATE BAHÁ'Í PROPERTY AREA ACQUIRED ADJACENT TO AND SOUTH OF PRESENT BOUNDARY OLIVE GROVE ENABLES SOUTHWEST QUADRANT GARDENS SURROUNDING MOST HOLY SHRINE BE COMPLETED... ALSO PURCHASED NEARLY 50,000 SQUARE METRES AGRICULTURAL LAND ADJACENT TO AND NORTH OF MAZRA'IH PROPERTY AS PROTECTION TO MANSION IN RAPIDLY DEVELOPING AREA.[61]
>
> UNIVERSAL HOUSE OF JUSTICE

After the passing of Shoghi Effendi in 1957, a contingent of Bahá'ís known collectively as the Hands of the Cause of God became the temporary chief stewards of the Bahá'í world. They supervised completion of the terracing and additional gardens at the Shrine of Bahá'u'lláh, as the Guardian had planned, and ensured that the standards of beauty, reverence, and care established by 'Abdu'l-Bahá, and Shoghi Effendi were upheld.

On April 21, 1963, one hundred years after Bahá'u'lláh's declaration in the fragrant rose-filled Garden of Riḍván in Baghdád, the election took place of the Universal House of Justice, the governing and legislative institution of the Bahá'í Faith decreed by Bahá'u'lláh in His *Kitáb-i-Aqdas*. Thereafter, plans to embellish and maintain the Bahá'í gardens in the Haifa-'Akká region were implemented under the direction of this institution. In 1966, work was begun on gardens located north of the main approach to the Shrine of Bahá'u'lláh, and in subsequent years, additional development of the gardens and acquisition of adjacent property were accomplished, as reflected in these cabled announcements from the Universal House of Justice to the Bahá'ís of the World.

The Universal House of Justice made known in its April 30, 1987, message to the Bahá'ís of the World that the time was auspicious for constructing additional administrative buildings on Mount Carmel and the monumental illuminated terraces beneath and above the Shrine of the Báb, as 'Abdu'l-Bahá had originally envisioned. Members of the worldwide Bahá'í community made sacrificial voluntary contributions to fund the historical project. After a decade, the new administrative buildings and the reshaping of Mount Carmel into magnificently landscaped and illuminated terraces and gardens were completed. Achievement of the epic project also further fulfilled Bahá'u'lláh's divine directive of more than a century past that Mount Carmel would be the site of the Báb's final resting place.

The terraces are designed principally to provide a majestic and contemplative approach through which Bahá'í pilgrims humbly and joyfully ascend Mount Carmel to pay homage to the Báb. The design also mirrors the Bahá'í standard of beauty and reverence for the resting places of the Báb and of Bahá'u'lláh, a perfect blending of spirit and nature inaugurated long ago by 'Abdu'l-Bahá, perpetuated by Shoghi Effendi, and continued today under direction of the Universal House of Justice.

The completed Bahá'í terraces and gardens on Mount Carmel were ceremoniously dedicated on May 22, 2001, before an invited audience of forty-five hundred people, including Bahá'ís from over one hundred eighty countries. The terraced gardens officially opened to the public about two weeks later, quickly becoming a major tourist attraction in Haifa. Nearly four million people have since visited the terraces, which are open to the public free of charge throughout the year, except on Bahá'í Holy Days. Organized, guided tours are also free and offered in a number of different languages.

As noted in background material released through the Bahá'í World Centre, the terraces span a kilometre and with the gardens cover approximately 200,000 square metres on the mountain.

The design of the terraces is profoundly symbolic spiritually and historically. The illumination pays homage to the Báb's imprisonment in Persia in the fortress of Máh-Kú during which at night he was denied even a lamp.

The nine terraced gardens above the Shrine of the Báb and the nine below it are a tribute to the Eighteen Letters of the Living, who were the first individuals to embrace the Báb's revelation in 1844. The terrace on which the Shrine of the Báb stands brings the total number to nineteen.

Planted on terrace nine directly below the Shrine are two sour orange trees which were cultivated and nurtured from seeds of an orange tree that grew in the courtyard of the house in which the Báb lived in Shíráz, Persia. These trees are reported to be in "robust health" by the Haifa Gardens Department at the Bahá'í World Centre.

"Water, both moving and still, is an integral element in the terraces' design, echoing the essential element found in traditional Persian gardens."

Anita R. Showers

Drawing on the Bahá'í spiritual principle of unity in diversity and the paradigm of the gardens designed by Shoghi Effendi, more than three hundred different types of plantings are used in the terraced gardens, many of them native to Israel. Lavender and rosemary, bougainvillaea, varieties of succulents, hedgings of santolina and duranta, and annual flowers such as pansies and geranium are planted in the gardens. Palm, flame, coral, olive, and evergreen trees, as well as flowering bulbs, bottle brush, and many other plantings augment the selections. The more formal garden areas are concentrated near the central stairway of the terraces, while the more informal gardens dominated by wildflowers and trees are planted on the periphery, offering refuge to indigenous birds and wildlife.

Water, both moving and still, is an integral element in the terraces' design, echoing the essential element found in traditional Persian gardens. The flight of stairs from the top of the terraces to the bottom is flanked by narrow watercourses, or runnels, in which water gently cascades down the mountain. The sound and movement soothes the senses while drowning the noise of Haifa's busy thoroughfares and nearby business and residential areas. Refreshing fountains and pools placed artistically throughout the terraces offer a refreshing reprieve from sun and heat. A large, star-shaped fountain encircled by sixteen pools of water, each one creating a glassy reflective surface, dominates the bottom or first terrace. Water is recycled in all of the fountains.[62]

Beyond the obvious splendor and serenity of the terraces and gardens is the stunning panorama that one sees of Haifa when standing on the terraces and looking northward to 'Akká, the city where Bahá'u'lláh was imprisoned. Equally spectacular when viewed at night, this vista is evocative of the following prophecy that 'Abdu'l-Bahá made in 1914 while in Haifa:

"In the future the distance between 'Akká and Haifa will be built up, and the two cities will join and clasp hands, becoming the two terminal sections of one mighty metropolis. As I look now over this scene, I see so clearly that it will become one of the first emporiums of the world. This great semi-circular bay will be transformed into the finest harbour, wherein the ships of all nations will seek shelter and refuge. The great vessels of all peoples will come to this port, bringing on their decks thousands and thousands of men and women from every part of the globe. The mountain and the plain will be dotted with the most modern buildings and palaces. Industries will be established and various institutions of philanthropic nature will be founded. The flowers of civilization and culture from all nations will be brought here to blend their fragrances together and blaze the way for the brotherhood of man. Wonderful gardens, orchards, groves and parks will be laid out on all sides. At night the great city will be lighted by electricity. The entire harbour from 'Akká to Haifa will be one path of illumination. Powerful searchlights will be placed on both sides of Mount Carmel to guide the steamers. Mount Carmel itself, from top to bottom, will be submerged in a sea of lights. A person standing on the summit of Mount Carmel, and the passengers of the steamers coming to it, will look upon the most sublime and majestic spectacle of the whole world."[63]

In addition to their aesthetic contribution to that "sublime and majestic spectacle," the Bahá'í garden terraces send a message of expectation and optimism to the peoples of the world. The Universal House of Justice echoed this hope in its statement read at the May 2001 dedication of the terraces:

"That our Earth has contracted into a neighborhood, no one can seriously deny. The world is being made new. Death pangs are yielding to birth pangs. The pain shall pass when members of the human race act upon the common recognition of their essential oneness. There is a light at the end of this tunnel of change beckoning humanity to the goal destined for it according to the testimonies recorded in all the Holy Books. The Shrine of the Báb stands as a symbol of the efficacy of that age-old promise, a sign of its urgency. It is, as well, a monument to the triumph of love over hate. The gardens which surround that structure, in their rich variety of colors and plants, are a reminder that the human race can live harmoniously in all its diversity. The light that shines from the central edifice is as a beacon of hope to the countless multitudes who yearn for a life that satisfies the soul as well as the body."[64]

"The entire harbour from Akká to Haifa will be one path of illumination… Mount Carmel itself, from top to bottom, will be submerged in a sea of lights."

———

'Abdu'l-Bahá

PART IV

Flowering in the Future

Garden in the inner courtyard and the south wing of the House of 'Abdu'lláh Páshá in 'Akká (Acre), Israel.

Historical photo of the inner courtyard of the House of 'Abdu'lláh Páshá, showing the stairs to the south wing where 'Abdu'l-Bahá resided with His family, in 'Akká (Acre), Israel.

Monument marking the resting place of Amatu'l-Bahá Rúhíyyih Khánum on Haparsim Street.

Since the official opening of the Bahá'í terraced gardens on Mount Carmel in 2001, new gardens at Bahá'í Holy Places in 'Akká and Haifa have been created and existing ones additionally beautified under the guidance and direction of the Universal House of Justice.

Refurbished in 2003 was the garden in the courtyard of the House of 'Abdu'lláh Páshá located in 'Akká. 'Abdu'l-Bahá moved His family to this property about four years after Bahá'u'lláh's passing. The Bahá'í World Centre restored the courtyard garden in the House of 'Abdu'lláh Páshá based upon its original design which can be clearly discerned in historical photographs. The restored garden was planted on the exact foundation of the original garden and included two new palm trees in the design. Bahá'í pilgrims have the privilege of visiting this perfectly arranged garden, which evokes the stories told by early pilgrims about 'Abdu'l-Bahá giving alms to the poor and greeting visitors.

Moreover, pilgrims have the honor of touring the House of 'Abdu'lláh Páshá, for it was there in early 1899 that 'Abdu'l-Bahá received the casket containing the Báb's sacred remains from its hiding place in Persia. He subsequently hid the remains for ten years in this house in His sister's room until the tomb of the Báb was completed and the remains interred by His own hand. Also in the House of 'Abdu'lláh Páshá, Shoghi Effendi, the future Guardian of the Bahá'í Faith, was born in March 1897, and may have played with other children in the original courtyard garden.

In recent years, gardens have been designed and created at Bahá'í properties located in Haifa along Haparsim Street, and the garden at the resting place of Amatu'l-Bahá Rúhíyyih Khánum, the wife of Shoghi Effendi, was completely landscaped in 2002.

In its annual letter to the Bahá'ís of the World, the Universal House of Justice in 2006 announced that the gardens around the Shrine of Bahá'u'lláh in Bahjí, at nearby Mazra'ih, and the Riḍván Garden would be further developed in the future.[65]

One area of the Haram-i-Aqdas (the outer sanctuary of the Shrine of Bahá'u'lláh comprising a quarter-circle of land) had been fully renovated by February 2007. The Junayn Gardens located north of Bahjí were completely restored by the following year along with a grove and modest farmhouse that Bahá'u'lláh, accompanied sometimes by family and friends, visited more than once during the final thirteen years of his life. Fresh red roses from the Junayn Gardens were, at Bahá'u'lláh's direction, given to each person in His presence during a festival and doubtless other occasions.*

With the acquisition of additional acreage that surrounds the Shrine of Bahá'u'lláh, plans were also being prepared for more enhancements to that sacred land, as announced in the spring of 2008 by the Universal House of Justice. Further, after more than two decades of negotiations, property had been secured within close proximity of the Riḍván Garden and the Mansion of Mazra'ih, Bahá'u'lláh's home after His departure from the prison-city of 'Akká.

At the Universal House of Justice's direction, the Riḍván Garden was undergoing major restoration in 2008. So fond was Bahá'u'lláh of this garden, that He wrote of it:

"…God's power and the perfection of His handiwork could enjoyably be seen in the blossoms, the fruits, the trees, the leaves and the streams," and He named it after the garden in Baghdád where He declared His mission in 1863. *The restoration includes "construction of a circulating water system, which will recreate the island frequented by Bahá'u'lláh, and the restoration of an antique flour mill, which was in use during His time."*[66]

This and other gardens at the Bahá'í Holy Places in Israel will continue to magnificently reflect the highest standards of beauty, reverence, and care instituted long ago by Bahá'u'lláh, 'Abdu'l-Bahá, and Shoghi Effendi. For the protection and oversight of these sacred properties, a deep sense of gratitude is owed to the Universal House of Justice and appreciation to the Bahá'í World Centre's gardening staff, which numbers more than 100 and is comprised of local workers and Bahá'í volunteers who hail from many different countries.

---

* *For details, see page 7.*

How befitting that in July 2008, the United Nations Education, Scientific, and Cultural Organization (UNESCO) inscribed the Bahá'í Holy Places and their majestic gardens to the list of World Heritage Sites – a list that includes The Great Wall of China, the Pyramids in Egypt and the Acropolis in Athens – international places deemed by UNESCO as having "outstanding" and "universal value to humanity."

Indeed, the Bahá'í terraces and gardens of the spirit in Haifa and 'Akká are intended for all of humanity. Through their beauty and cohesive design, their peacefulness and dignity, they offer a symbolic glimpse into what Bahá'ís believe is destined to be – a spiritualized planet, a humanity unified in its diversity, flowering to its fullest, and exemplifying Bahá'u'lláh's timeless words: "Ye are the fruits of one tree, and the leaves of one branch." [67]

References

Preface

01. Amir Gilat, "A world's wonder in the heart of Haifa," published in the Hebrew language newspaper *Ma'ariv*, 18 July 2000, cited in Bahá'í World News Service, "Reshaping 'God's holy mountain' to create a vision of peace and beauty for all humanity," 30 November 2000.
02. Bahá'í World News Service, "Travel writers salute 'floral jewel'," 1 February 2004.
03. Bahá'u'lláh, *The Hidden Words*, (Persian) no. 33.
04. Penelope Hobhouse, *The Story of Gardening*, p. 63.
05. Mehdi Khansari, M. Reza Moghtader, and Minouch Yavari, *The Persian Garden: Echoes of Paradise*, p. 17.

Story of the Gardens at the Bahá'í Holy Places

01. 'Abdu'l-Bahá, cited in J. E. Esslemont, *Bahá'u'lláh and the New Era*, p. 23.; The spoken chronicle of Munírih Khánum, in Lady Blomfield, *The Chosen Highway*, p. 85; The spoken chronicle of Túbá Khánum, in ibid., p. 95.
02. Mary Perkins, *Servant of the Glory: The Life of 'Abdu'l-Bahá*, p. 6.
03. 'Alí-Akbar Furútan, comp. and ed., *Stories of Bahá'u'lláh*, (Tablet of 'Abdu'l-Bahá to Bashír-i-Ilahí, 16 Dhi'l-Hijjah, AH 1337), p. 5.
04. Bahíyyih Khánum, in *Bahíyyih Khánum: The Greatest Holy Leaf. A compilation from Bahá'í sacred texts and writings of the Guardian of the Faith and Bahíyyih Khánum's own letters Compiled by the Research Department at the Bahá'í World Centre*, p. 42; The spoken chronicle of Bahíyyih Khánum, in Lady Blomfield, *The Chosen Highway*, p. 40.
05. Bahá'u'lláh, *Tablets of Bahá'u'lláh*, p. 142.
06. ibid., p. 164.
07. 'Abdu'l-Bahá, *The Promulgation of Universal Peace*, p. 295.
08. 'Abdu'l-Bahá, *Bahá'í World Faith* (Section II – Words of 'Abdu'l-Bahá), p. 267.
09. Bahá'u'lláh, cited in Shoghi Effendi, *The World Order of Bahá'u'lláh*, p. 135.
10. Tarázu'lláh Samandarí, *Moments With Bahá'u'lláh: Memoirs of the Hand of the Cause of God*, pp. 54-55.
11. Such was the experience of the author and some fellow Bahá'ís who were on pilgrimage at the Bahá'í Holy Places from March 28 to April 5, 2005. The pilgrim guide offered that not everyone who enters the rooms detects the rose scent.
12. Bahá'u'lláh, cited in Shoghi Effendi, *God Passes By*, pp. 101-02.
13. For a comprehensive account on Bahá'u'lláh's Writings and Utterances, see *The Revelation of Bahá'u'lláh*, volumes 1-4, by Adib Taherzadeh, published by George Ronald.
14. Bahá'u'lláh, *Gleanings from the Writings of Bahá'u'lláh*, XIV.
15. Nabíl, cited in Shoghi Effendi, *God Passes By*, p. 153.
16. Shoghi Effendi, *God Passes By*, pp. 170-71.
17. H. M. Balyuzi, *Bahá'u'lláh: The King of Glory*, p. 226.
18. ibid., p. 235.
19. Adib Taherzadeh, *The Revelation of Bahá'u'lláh*, vol. 2, p. 241.
20. Shoghi Effendi, *God Passes By*, p. 192.
21. 'Abdu'l-Bahá, cited in Esslemont, *Bahá'u'lláh and the New Era*, pp. 33-34.
22. Taherzadeh, *The Revelation of Bahá'u'lláh*, vol. 4, p. 7.
23. The spoken chronicle of Túbá Khánum, in Blomfield, *Chosen Highway*, p. 97.
24. Bahá'u'lláh, cited in Taherzadeh, *Revelation* 4, p. 15.
25. ibid., pp. 11-12.
26. Blomfield, *Chosen Highway*, p. 96.
27. May Maxwell, *An Early Pilgrimage*, pp. 32-34.
28. Ugo Giachery, *Shoghi Effendi: Recollections*, pp. 109-10.
29. Taherzadeh, *Revelation* 4, p. 114.
30. Balyuzi, *King of Glory*, p. 363-64.
31. Giachery, *Recollections*, pp. 110-11.
32. The Báb, *Selections from the Writings of the Báb*, p. 87.
33. Giachery, *Recollections*, p. 111.
34. 'Abdu'l-Bahá, quoted in Rúhíyyih Rabbání, *The Priceless Pearl*, p. 21.
35. 'Abdu'l-Bahá, quoted in ibid., p. 5.
36. Rúhíyyih Rabbání, *The Priceless Pearl*, pp. 86-87.
37. Giachery, *Recollections*, pp. 79-80.
38. ibid., pp. 112-13.
39. Bahá'í World Centre, "A new system of irrigation for the Terraces," in *Vineyard of the Lord: Mount Carmel Bahá'í Projects Update*, No. 9, 'Azamat 152 BE/May 1995 AD, pp. 5-6.
40. Amatu'l-Bahá Rúhíyyih Khánum, "The Completion of the International Archives," in *The Bahá'í World* 13 (1954-1963): 403.
41. Rabbání, *Priceless Pearl*, p. 265.
42. Khánum, "The Completion of the International Archives," in *The Bahá'í World* 13 (1954-1963): 425.
43. Taherzadeh, *The Covenant of Bahá'u'lláh*, p. 191.
44. Amatu'l-Bahá Rúhíyyih Khánum, cited in Violette Nakhjavani, *Amatu'l-Bahá Visits India*, p. 159.
45. Giachery, *Recollections*, pp. 123-24.
46. ibid., pp. 127-29.
47. Rabbání, *Priceless Pearl*, p. 88.
48. ibid., pp. 88-89.
49. Giachery, *Recollections*, pp. 130-31.
50. Rabbání, *Priceless Pearl*, p. 234.
51. ibid., p. 143.
52. ibid., p. 84.
53. Giachery, *Recollections*, pp. 217-19.
54. ibid., pp. 119-20.
55. Rabbání, *Priceless Pearl*, p. 84.
56. ibid., p. 34.
57. Giachery, *Recollections*, p. 117.
58. ibid., p. 118.
59. Universal House of Justice, "World Center Developments – Erection of Obelisk and Extension of Gardens," 13 December 1971 (No. 105.1), in *Messages From the Universal House of Justice, 1963-1986, The Third Epoch of the Formative Age*, p. 209.
60. Universal House of Justice, "Extension of Gardens at Bahjí," 4 December 1973 (No. 139.1), in ibid., p. 258.
61. Universal House of Justice, "Property Acquisitions in Holy Land," 24 September 1980 (Nos. 264.1, 264.2 and 264.3), in ibid., p. 462.
62. Bahá'í Office of Public Information, "Terraces of the Shrine of the Báb," May 2001.
63. 'Abdu'l-Bahá, cited in Esslemont, *Bahá'u'lláh and the New Era*, pp. 228-29.
64. Universal House of Justice, "On the Occasion of the Official Opening of the Terraces of the Shrine of the Báb," May 22, 2001, in *The Bahá'í World 2001-2002*, p. 66.
65. Universal House of Justice, *Riḍván 2006 Message to the Bahá'ís of the World*, April 2006.
66. Universal House of Justice, *Letter to all National Spiritual Assemblies*, May 12, 2008.
67. Bahá'u'lláh, *Tablets of Bahá'u'lláh*, p. 164.

Bibliography

'Abdu'l-Bahá. *Bahá'í World Faith: Selected Writings of Bahá'u'lláh and 'Abdu'l-Bahá (Section II – Words of 'Abdu'l-Bahá)*. Wilmette, IL: Bahá'í Publishing Trust, 1976.

— *The Promulgation of Universal Peace: Talks Delivered by 'Abdu'l-Bahá during His Visit to the United States and Canada in 1912*. 2nd ed. Compiled by Howard MacNutt. Wilmette, IL: Bahá'í Publishing Trust, 1982.

The Báb. *Selections from the Writings of the Báb*. Haifa: Bahá'í World Centre, 1982.

Bahá'í Office of Public Information. "Terraces of the Shrine of the Báb." Haifa: Bahá'í World Centre, May 2001. Available at http://www.bahaiworldnews.org/terraces/terraces.en.html.

Bahá'í World Centre. "A new system of irrigation for the Terraces." In *Vineyard of the Lord: Mount Carmel Bahá'í Projects Update*. No. 9. Haifa: Bahá'í World Centre, 'Azamat 152 BE/May 1995 AD.

Bahá'í World News Service. "Reshaping 'God's holy mountain' to create a vision of peace and beauty for all humanity." Haifa: Bahá'í World Centre, 30 November 2000. Available at http://news.bahai.org/story.cfm?storyid=79.

— "Travel writers salute 'floral jewel'." Haifa: Bahá'í World Centre, 1 February 2004. Available at http://news.bahai.org/story.cfm?storyid=276.

Bahá'u'lláh. *Gleanings from the Writings of Bahá'u'lláh*. 1st pocket-size ed. Translated by Shoghi Effendi. Wilmette, IL: Bahá'í Publishing Trust, 1983.

— *The Hidden Words*. Translated by Shoghi Effendi with the assistance of some English friends. Wilmette, IL: Bahá'í Publishing Trust, Reprinted 1990.

— *Tablets of Bahá'u'lláh revealed after the Kitáb-i-Aqdas*. Compiled by the Research Department of the Universal House of Justice and translated by Habib Taherzadeh with the assistance of a Committee at the Bahá'í World Centre. Haifa: Bahá'í World Centre, 1978.

Bahíyyih Khánum: The Greatest Holy Leaf. A compilation from Bahá'í sacred texts and writings of the Guardian of the Faith and Bahíyyih Khánum's own letters. Compiled by the Research Department at the Bahá'í World Centre. Haifa: Bahá'í World Centre, 1982.

Balyuzi, H. M. *Bahá'u'lláh: The King of Glory*. Oxford: George Ronald, 1980.

Blomfield, Lady (Sitárih Khánum). *The Chosen Highway*. Wilmette, IL: Bahá'í Publishing Trust, 1967.

Esslemont, J. E. *Bahá'u'lláh and the New Era*. rev. 4th ed. London: The Bahá'í Publishing Trust, 1974.

Furútan, 'Alí-Akbar, comp. and ed. *Stories of Bahá'u'lláh*. Translated by Katayoon and Robert Crerar. Oxford: George Ronald, 1990.

Giachery, Ugo. *Shoghi Effendi: Recollections*. Oxford: George Ronald, 1973.

Gilat, Amir. "A world's wonder in the heart of Haifa." In the Hebrew language newspaper *Ma'ariv* (Tel Aviv), 18 July 2000.

Hobhouse, Penelope. *The Story of Gardening*. London: Dorling Kindersley Limited, 2002.

Khansari, Mehdi, Reza M. Moghtader, and Minouch Yavari. *The Persian Garden: Echoes of Paradise*. Washington, DC: Wage Publishers, 2004.

Maxwell, May. *An Early Pilgrimage*. Oxford: George Ronald, 1969.

Momen, Wendi, gen. ed. *A Basic Bahá'í Dictionary*. Oxford: George Ronald, 1989.

Nakhjavani, Violette. *Amatu'l-Bahá Visits India*. New Delhi: Bahá'í Publishing Trust, n.d.

Perkins, Mary. *Servant of The Glory. The Life of 'Abdu'l-Bahá*. Oxford: George Ronald, 1999.

Rabbani, Rúhíyyih. *The Priceless Pearl*. London: Bahá'í Publishing Trust, 1969.

Samandarí, Tarázu'lláh. *Moments With Bahá'u'lláh: Memoirs of the Hand of the Cause of God Tarázu'lláh Samandarí*. Translated by Mehdi Samandari and Marzieh Gail. Los Angeles: Kalimát Press, 1995.

Shoghi Effendi. *God Passes By*. Rev. ed. Wilmette, IL: Bahá'í Publishing Trust, 1974.

— *The World Order of Bahá'u'lláh: Selected Letters*. Wilmette, IL: Bahá'í Publishing Trust, 1982.

Taherzadeh, Adib. *The Covenant of Bahá'u'lláh*. Oxford: George Ronald, 1992.

— *The Revelation of Bahá'u'lláh*. Vol. 2. Oxford: George Ronald, 1977.

— *The Revelation of Bahá'u'lláh*. Vol. 4. Oxford: George Ronald, 1987.

Universal House of Justice. *The Bahá'í World*. Vol. 13, (1954-1963). Haifa, Israel: Bahá'í World Centre, 1970.

— *The Bahá'í World 2001-2002*. Haifa, Israel: Bahá'í World Centre, 2003.

— *Letter to all National Spiritual Assemblies*. Haifa, Israel: Bahá'í World Centre, May 12, 2008.

— *Messages From the Universal House of Justice, 1963-1986, The Third Epoch of the Formative Age*. Geoffrey W. Marks, Compiler. Wilmette, IL: Bahá'í Publishing Trust, 1996.

— *Ridván 2006 Message to the Bahá'ís of the World*. Haifa, Israel: Bahá'í World Centre, April 2006.

Index

A

'Abbás 4
'Abdu'l-'Azíz 20
'Abdu'l-Bahá 3, 5, 6, 7, 10, 30, 36, 37, 42, 48, 50, 61, 70, 77, 78, 90, 115, 116, 120, 134, 141, 142
'Abdu'lláh Páshá 140, 141
Abraham 5
Abu'l-Qásim 37
Abu-Sinan 39
Adib Taherzadeh 20, 24, 39, 77
Adrianople 19, 20
'Akká xiii, 10, 20, 24, 30, 36, 37, 48, 49, 70, 73, 77, 97, 100, 104, 134, 141, 142, 143
Alburz 3
Amatu'l-Bahá Rúhíyyih Khánum 61, 141, 149
Arabic 15
Asíyih Khánum 3, 6

B

Báb xiv, 5, 6, 11, 14, 15, 48, 49, 50, 61, 70, 116, 120, 141
Babylon 14
Baghdád 10, 14, 15, 19, 30, 115, 142
Bahá'í Holy Days 16, 120
Bahá'í Holy Places xvii, 10, 36, 49, 50, 73, 100, 141, 142, 143
Bahá'í International Archives 73
Bahá'í World Centre xiii, 36, 42, 49, 70, 100, 120, 142
Bahá'u'lláh xiv, 3, 4, 5, 7, 10, 14, 15, 16, 19, 20, 23, 24, 30, 36, 37, 39, 42, 48, 49, 50, 61, 77, 78, 90, 97, 115, 116, 120, 134, 141, 142, 143
Bahíyyih Khánum 3, 4, 6
Bahjí 10, 77, 84, 90, 100, 101, 104, 109, 142
Black Pit 11
Book of Certitude 14
Buddha 5
Buq'atu'l-Hamra' 39
Bustan-i-Kabir 39

C

Canada 10
Carrara 109
Caspian Sea 3
China xiv
Constantinople 15, 19
Czar Alexander II 23

D

Dr. Habib Mu'ayyad 77

E

Edirne 19
Egypt xiv
Emperor Franz Joseph 23
Emperor Napoleon III 20
England 104
Europe 10, 109
Exalted Leaf 6

F

Fars xiv
Festival of Ridván 16
Fí amánu'lláh 7
Firdaws 39

G

Garden of Najíb Páshá 15
Garden of Najíbíyyih 15
Garden of Na'mayn 30
Garden of Ridván 15, 16, 30, 36, 37, 39, 115
Greatest Holy Leaf 6
Guardian of the Bahá'í Faith 50

H

Hafez 11
Haifa xiii, 10, 48, 73, 84, 100, 101, 104, 115, 120, 131, 134, 141, 143
Hájí Mírzá Haydar-'Alí 77
Hands of the Cause of God 115
Haparsim Street 141
Haram-i-Aqdas 84, 90, 142
H.M. Balyuzi 19, 39
Holy Land 94, 100
House of 'Abbúd 97
House of 'Abdu'lláh Páshá 141

I

India xiv, 77
Iran xiv
Iraq xiv
Islam xiv
Israel xiv, 20, 70, 100, 142
Istanbul 15

J

Jesus 5
Junayna 7
Junayn Gardens 142
Junaynih 39

K

Kaiser Wilhelm I 23
Khadíjih-Bagnum 6
Kitáb-i-Aqdas 23, 115
Krishna 5

L

Leroy Ioas 73
Letters of the Living 120
London 94

M

Ma'ariv *xiii*
Maghreb *xiv*
Máh-Kú *50, 120*
Mansion of Bahjí *37, 39, 42, 77, 78, 84, 91, 94*
Mansion of Mazra'ih *24, 30, 142*
Master's Tea House *100*
Mázindarán *3*
Mazra'ih *24, 37, 39, 142*
Mírza Mahmúd-i-Kashání *19*
Mírzá Mihdí *3, 6, 23*
Mírza Muhammad-Qulí *19*
Monument Gardens *70, 73*
Moses *5*
Most Mighty Branch *6*
Most Sacred Spot *84*
Mount Carmel *xiii, 10, 48, 49, 50, 70, 73, 116, 120, 134, 141*
Mt. Carmel *84*
Muhammad *5*
Muhammad Páshá Safwat *24*
Munírih Khánum *3*
Muradíyyih *19*
Murgh-Mahallín *4*

N

Nabíl *16*
Na'mayn River *30*
Napoleon III *23*
Napoleon's Hill *39*
Násirí'd-Dín Sháh *20*
Navváb *6*

O

Ottoman *19*
Ottoman authorities *24*
Ottoman empire *19*

P

Persia *xiv, 3, 10, 11, 14, 48, 50, 120*
Persian *4, 11, 14, 37, 131*
Pilgrim House *100*
Pope Pius IX *23*
Purest Branch *6*

Q

Qiblih *42, 85*
Queen Victoria *23*

R

Rída Big *19*
Ridván Garden *30, 84, 142*
Rosa damascena *36*
Rúhíyyih Khánum *70*
Rúhíyyih Rabbaní *61, 73, 77, 90, 94, 97, 101*

S

Samaríyyih *39*
Sea of Galilee *104*
Shí'ih *11, 48*
Shíráz *11, 120*
Shoghi Effendi *xiv, 23, 37, 39, 42, 49, 50, 61, 73, 77, 78, 84, 85, 90, 97, 100, 109, 115, 120, 131, 141, 142*
Shrine of Bahá'u'lláh *10, 37, 42, 84, 91, 97, 115, 142*
Shrine of the Báb *10, 37, 49, 50, 61, 70, 84, 97, 109, 120, 134*
Síyáh-Chál *11, 14*
Sultán of Turkey *15, 20*

T

Tablet of Carmel *73*
Tablet of the Branch *7*
Tabríz *11*
Takur *3*
Tall-i-Fakhkhar *39*
'Taráz Effendi *7*
Tarázu'lláh Samandarí *7*
The Bahá'í World Centre *141*
The Covenant of Bahá'u'lláh *77*
The Garden of Hájí Báqir *4*
The Hidden Words *14*
The Sultan of Turkey *20*
Tigris River *14, 15*
Tihrán *3, 11*
Túbá Khánum *3, 30, 36*
Turkey *xiv, 15*

U

Ugo Giachery *37, 49, 50, 61, 66, 70, 78, 91, 97, 100, 104, 109*
UNESCO *143*
United Nations *143*
United States *10*
Universal House of Justice *115, 116, 120, 134, 141, 142*

Y

Yirkih *39*

Z

Zoroaster *5*

Further Information

Visit www.ganbahai.org.il for more information about tours of the Bahá'í Shrines and gardens in Haifa and 'Akká.